ONE MORE STORY TO TELL

A Crash Course on Writing Personal and Family Histories

by
Jason Lee

Jason Lee

TABLE OF CONTENTS

TABLE OF CONTENTS CONTINUED

SPECIAL THANKS

This book couldn't have been made without the help of all of the people who supported me through its production. This includes Nathan Anderson, and Kirk Duncan for their inspiration and financial support. I would also be remiss if I forgot to mention my parents and in-laws who were incredibly patient with me during the writing. The book, notebook, and quill symbols are used under a creative commons license and were designed by Marco Galtarossa, Noémi Farkas, and Hea Poh Lin respectively. Last, and most important is my beautiful wife, without whom this book would never have even been a thought in my head, let alone in your hands.

Jason Lee

PART 1

SO YOU WANT TO WRITE A BOOK...

Jason Lee

1

BEHIND THE MASK OF THE MAN CALLED DAD

When I was 19, I went on a trip for two years to South America. Due to the nature of what I was doing, I didn't get very regular contact with my family, or anyone that I knew before. There were times when I was one of 10 Norteamericanos (North Americans) in an Andean city of less than 50,000, and I was the only one for hundreds of miles with blonde hair and blue eyes. I was learning a whole new culture, a whole new language, and a whole new side of who I was. Yet, it was in this strange town, in the top of the Andes that I first cracked the surface and met the person my father really was.

I had managed to find my way to an internet cafe in the little town of Espinar, Peru, and had paid a fee to use one of their old, tired computers. They weren't good for much, but they were more than adequate for email.

On this particular day, I logged in and plugged in my big, 8GB portable hard drive into the USB port to try and upload a few pictures to send home to my family. It was an excruciatingly slow process, but eventually I got a couple ready to send. I spend a few more minutes writing home about what I had been up to for the last week since I was able to email them last. I made a couple of shoutouts to people I knew my dad was forwarding my emails to and then sent it off.

With the last 5 minutes I had before my hour was up, I paid a few extra centimos and printed off the email my dad had sent so I could read it at home, without having to pay for the time. Then, I logged off the computer, carefully folded up the page from my dad and put it in my pocket, and a friend and I both went back to the small rooftop apartment we were renting.

When we got inside, I pulled out the sheet of paper and began reading. And, I was stunned.

Getting emails from my parents wasn't uncommon. I knew that they would write me every single day if it didn't cost so much to print things off down there. But usually, there was a tone that came implicit with the emails.

It was a parental tone. Not a bad, scolding type or anything like that. In fact, up until this email, I would have told you that it was just who my parents were. It was the tone that says, we're here for you and proud of you. Keep up the good work. Have you tried doing this… or that? You know. The kind of things parents say to their kids.

But, this one was different.

This email wasn't written by my dad. It was written by Kelly. The man who loved my mom. The person who grew up in a broken home in Tooele, UT. It was written by the person who lived underneath the title "father."

He wrote about how he had been talking with an old friend from high school, and remembered the times they had spent together. He told me about the times that they

~5~

had gone up into the mountains and taken their rifles, sleeping bags, and my dad's guitar, all thrown in the back of his old pick-up truck. They would get some girls and go up and sing songs around the campfire. Songs by Neil Diamond; or James Taylor; or Peter, Paul, and Mary.

I don't know if I had just been too young to hear these stories earlier, or if he had simply never told them. What I do know is that for the first time, I had connected with my dad as a person, and it was powerful.

And it all happened because he decided to write a few stories down. Even though writing like that might have been hard for him, it meant the world to me. I know what it will mean to the ones you are writing for.

To start this whole thing off, there is something you should know: writing a book is not a small task, or a weekend project. And so, while I will often use words like easy, and simple, it is important to understand that writing a book is still going to be a lot of work. There's no getting around that. You will spend a lot of time on it. You will have to rewrite and edit a lot of it. And, just when you think it's done, you will have to go to what will feel like some pretty big lengths to get it published. It's all part of the process. But, that process is not necessarily difficult.

More importantly, it will all be worth it. Both to you and to those who will come to know your stories through your writing.

The book in your hands has one simple purpose: to help you write your stories so that people read them. In the chapters that follow, you'll learn some of the tricks that the professionals use to make their writing exciting and engaging. You'll find that writing a book isn't nearly as hard as you might have thought, and that the world of the internet makes it easy to get it published.

2

THE PROCESS

My name is Jason, and while I didn't start to understand my dad until I was almost 20, he was the one who taught me how to write on countless nights when a big school paper was due the next day.

I was tired, and he was tired, but the paper wasn't done yet.

You see, I was one of those kids who liked to procrastinate my homework as long as possible. If we had three weeks to do the project, you could bet that I would casually mention it to my parents the night before it was due. I would get stressed, and they would get mad, asking why I hadn't done anything with it so far. Then, we would scramble to see if we could actually accomplish it.

Sometimes, that meant late night trips to Wal-Mart to see if we could cobble together a science experiment that we could perform before the next morning. Other times, it meant research and crafting for whatever art piece was supposed to accompany the research. But most often, it meant writing. It would go something like this:

At five or six in the afternoon, I would mention that I needed to get on the computer to do my homework.

"What homework?" they would ask.

"I have a paper due tomorrow that I need to work on," I would reply, trying not to raise any suspicion.

"Have you started it yet?" would come the inevitable, worried question.

And then, I would try to work out some excuse to make it sound easier than it was. "Not yet, but it's really easy," I

~10~

might say, or "Yeah, I just need to finish it up."

No matter what excuse I came up with, the night would end up about the same.

I would go down and slave away at the computer, trying to make up for weeks worth of research and writing in a few hours. Then, around 8 at night as my siblings were getting into bed, I would come up exhausted with a first draft I thought was a final draft, and hand it proudly to my dad.

I thought for the longest time that my dad was an English major. That was probably because my father had an eagle's eye for cutting through the fluff and catching my mistakes. At the time, I considered it a curse. He would mark up the page with one of his nice red Uniball pens and hand it back, usually with a few penetrating questions about what exactly was the point, and whether or not I actually knew what I was talking about. It felt like he had been there watching over my shoulder to see what bits I actually knew and what bits I had made up. Double spacing only made things worse because it gave him more space to correct.

And then I would watch jealously as my sisters went to sleep before I returned to stare at the large white computer monitor for another hour, carefully correcting my mistakes. Every draft I finished I thought was the one that would make it through the piercing gaze, but more often than not, they ended in more red pen.

By the time midnight rolled around, I would usually have a paper that my dad would consider passable, although to this day, I'm not sure if it was because it was actually good, or he was just too tired to care anymore. Then, we would both crawl into bed, exhausted.

In elementary school, I thought that my writing was just bad, and it probably was. But, as time went on, I noticed that he would stay up pretty predictably until midnight or one in the morning before calling the paper good. I knew I was improving, but it seemed like my writing was never quite good enough. It could always be a little bit clearer, or a little bit more accurate, at least until he got tired enough that we could go to bed.

I've since learned that it's just part of my dad's character. Where other kid's dads would make their pinewood derby car for them, hoping to help them win, my dad would stand there and tell me what to do, insisting that I learn to do it for myself. He would show me where to cut, where to sand, and then go inside to let me do the work.

You'd think I'd learn, by the time high school rolled around, to finish my projects early, but procrastination ingrained in me by one simple fact: my process worked. Those super intensive nights spent pouring over my papers resulted in very high grades on those papers. And, when I arrived at college, I realized to my surprise that I was a remarkably better writer than the others around me.

In hindsight, it wasn't that I had actually had that much more raw talent than the rest of them. I just spent so much time in that hyper-focused state that my writing couldn't help but improve. It wasn't the procrastination that had made me good, either. It was being willing to write, and then rewrite until I got it *all* right.

My first job out of college was writing for a research firm, taking their dry statistical reports and attempting to transform them into something more exciting to read. My second was writing for an events company. No matter where I was writing or who I was writing for, I found one common thread: people liked how I wrote about them. They called it a gift, or a talent, but I knew the truth.

In the end, I can only attribute my ability to write to hours upon hours of dedicated practice with an even more dedicated father helping me to improve.

I've written a lot of stories, about a lot of people. And I've learned that there are some pretty easy tips and tricks that I've learned along the way that help make writing worth reading. I want to help you turn your life stories into a meaningful, engaging book that will stand as a testament to your life. And believe it or not, you've already seen an example of it at work.

You see, in introducing myself, I could have created a list of accomplishments. I could have listed places and people and figures, but interesting writing is much more than a list of events.

It's about stories!

So as you start to read this book, and begin writing your own, one of the key pieces to it all is to begin to think in terms of stories. Watch for my examples, and how I have actually written this book. It is meant to serve as an example as well as a set of instructions.

I want to walk you through the steps of taking a collection of stories, whether they are your own or your ancestors, and crafting them to be memorable and meaningful. This will mean a first, rough draft. Next you will go through editing, working and reworking your words to get them better. When you have edited more than you thought you could, you will move on to getting your book laid out, so that it actually looks like a book. Then is the trick of getting it published.

None of these steps is terribly difficult. They might be time-consuming, or even emotionally draining. But, they are worth the effort.

When you tell a story, you leave a little bit of yourself behind in the words. When you give someone your book, it's like giving them a small window into your soul. And when you write about someone who has already passed on, you allow someone else to reach out and shake their hand, even if it's just for a moment. Books and written stories are powerful in ways that we are only beginning to understand. They can change lives and educate in ways that nothing else can. They are records of history, and tales of sadness and triumph.

By writing your own book, you join the ranks of history, and the countless others who have helped to shape the world we now live it. Welcome to the club.

3

<u>Who are you?</u>

Who are you?

I want you to think about that for a sec. No one is created in a void. You are a miraculous, unique combination of events, circumstances, and people. You are the result of thousands of years of history, mixed with a dash of ineffable something people call personality, or soul, or some other word. It's really quite a thing to be you.

You have a story.

But, your story is, in part, made up of the stories of many other people. In other words, there is a question that lies implicit with every attempt at describing yourself:

Who made you who you are?

I want you to think about this for a second. Who are your friends and mentors? Who are your parents? Their parents? Your ancestors? How did their decisions make a difference in your life?

If you are reading this in English, then somewhere along the way, one of your ancestors picked up the language. Depending on your heritage, they might have learned it in hopes to use it in trade, or science. Or maybe, you go back even further to those who helped invent the language as a low class German trying to learn the upper class's French, resulting in the strange combination that we speak today.

If you're reading this in America, chances are that your ancestors didn't originate here. One of them, at one point in time, made the decision to leave their home to go somewhere they had only heard about.

Do you know the stories of these people? Why do you think the way you do about religion, philosophy, politics, or earning a living?

What blood flows through your veins?

In a world where opposing opinions split every hair, words are cheap. But you are a living testament to the principles lived by your ancestors. Some might have needed changing. Some have had a powerful effect on making you a better person.

Today, there is a massive amount of information available to help you discover exactly who you are. Huge databases funnel into family history websites, opening new insights into the past. This is an incredible opportunity for those who take advantage of it.

However, in my experience, this research ends up in one of two paths:

Proof of Existence

My friend Jared has dedicated hours of his free time to one thing: graveyards. He has created a website database that collects the names and dates off of tombstones from graveyards around the world and puts them in a format where they can be searched easily.

His efforts have made a great resource that has answered questions for those looking for the proof of their ancestors. Similar resources are being compiled on a daily basis to digitize census records and municipal records. Each one provides a piece of the puzzle that was someone's life. There's just one issue:

All of the records provide little more than proof that the ancestor existed. When you go back to see who they actually were, you are left with a blank. You know that they were born, because of a number on a gravestone and the fact that you exist at all. You assume that the person must have reproduced at some point in their life, again taking your existence as the proof. With a little bit of detective work, you can even see their children and maybe when they got married. But the records are vague. They are simple. The picture is incomplete.

Too Much Information

Occasionally, you'll find the exact opposite. It usually comes because someone kept a journal or was involved in a high profile event. For whatever the reason, the situation suddenly flips.

Whereas before, the ancestor was almost a line item in your family history index, a journal suddenly gives you exponentially more information about one person than about everyone else around them. This tends to be the case to the point where journals are used to help confirm events in the lives of the people they lived around. And while there are those that enjoy combing through the crumbling handwritten pages, it is way too much information for the average person to try and get through.

The volumes of journal become a burden that require more work just to understand. The stories that matter have been buried in the volumes of day to day monotonies. I have ancestors who crossed the plains of the American West as pioneers. They wrote in their journals everyday, recording bits and pieces of their life and the hardships they endure. Luckily for me, after over a hundred years, people have sifted through the records and condensed them into a few powerful stories that help me know what kind of people they were.

Unfortunately, I don't have the luxury of waiting for every set of journals to be combed through and abridged through the hundred year process. There are ancestors whose journals have been taken by different branches of the family, leaving me in the same situation.

I wish someone had written it all into a book.

I wish that someone had taken the time to make it into a powerful book that I can use to help inspire me and my family. But, I also know that I can help that process happen today. Genealogy is often looked at as a study of the past, but we can record the important stories of tomorrow, today.

We can write the books that our descendants will treasure. The torch has been passed to us to make more than another record for tomorrow's historians. We must create better stories.

THE MEMOIR

A memoir is defined in the dictionary as "a record of events written by a person having intimate knowledge of them and based on personal observation."

The word itself comes from the French word mémoire which comes from the Latin word memoria. Both of those words mean the same thing: memory. Have you every heard of someone "writing their memoirs?" Memoirs is just the plural form, and is usually used to describe when someone records their personal experiences, kind of like an autobiography.

But that being said, there's a big difference between a biography and someone's memoirs. The first can be volumes long, and tend to be chronological and drawn out in nature. Their aim usually seems to be to give an exact account (or at least as exact as can be had) of the person's life. They often include the perspectives of others and an anchoring in specific times and places.

A memoir is something more than just the facts and figures, or the dates and data that could be found on a Wikipedia article. They are often shorter, but they put in emotion that brings the stories to life. What I am looking for in a memoir is an introduction, a window into who you are. I want to climb inside your head and see through your eyes. I want to walk the proverbial mile in your moccasins and know the real you. And that is the type of story I'm going to teach you to write.

So let's redefine the term so it's a little easier, shall we?

Memoir: a set of stories that shows the world who the author really is, and what they stand for.

Did you know that some of the most influential books

of all literature were written as memoirs? James Joyce, a celebrated modernist wrote *A Portrait of the Artist as a Young Man* originally as a long autobiography and then later went back to shorten it. In high school, I was required to read *The Things They Carried*, a semi-biographical novel that tells about the author, Tim O'Brien's experiences in Vietnam.

Even today, many of the compelling books on the New York Times Bestseller list are books that tell the true stories of people who grew up all around the world. *The Glass Castle*, by Jeannette Walls is a great example of a modern author who told a powerful story through her own memoirs.

In order to teach you how to write this type of book, I'm going to have to introduce you to an often overlooked genre of writing called Creative Nonfiction. It should also be noted that you can write this way even if you weren't there for the events. You can, and should, apply these techniques to the idea of writing a family history as well.

At first glance, this might seem like a bit of a contradiction. I mean, if it's nonfiction, the events are set, right? Not a whole lot of wiggle room in there for creativity, or so it would seem. But, the art of creative nonfiction is not just about the facts. It's about which facts to use, and how to use them, and in what order. It's about how you express those facts, and most importantly, how to make them interesting. You see, there are multiple ways to tell the same story, and each way can help us understand it differently. This applies equally, whether you are writing your own story, or that of someone else.

Imagine for an instant a simple story. The following is a very "fact-based" way of telling a story:

> *John is a 14 year old boy living in Colorado. John has been asked by his mother to get a loaf of bread from the store. He walks to the story and buys the bread. He returns home after buying it and gives the bread to his mom. John's mom is happy and gives him a reward. John learned that his mom appreciated what he did.*

If all I did were to give you those facts, you would barely even consider it a story. It's boring. There's no point to it. There's not climax. It's just an everyday occurrence that happened to an everyday sort of boy.

But, what if you took those facts and you worked on how you used them? What if you changed the order of them? What if you played with the way that you said it? What if, instead of that sad excuse for a story, it started like this:

> *John never would have thought that a loaf of Wonderbread would be so important. But then, John had never really been interested in helping his mom much, either...*

Would you want to read more? Creative nonfiction uses the tricks of writing fiction, and applies them to history.

This is important. I'm not just teaching you how to write stories. I'm teaching you how to write stories *people want to read*. Those are two different things.

But what if you don't think you have a great story about Wonderbread? Believe me when I say that no one is so boring that they don't have a good story or two. If you are wondering whether or not you have any, I would ask one question: have you ever been stressed?

Think about it for a second. Stress, whether it resulted in something or not, is one of the driving points for any story. It denotes conflict, drama, and emotion. And those are the things you need to write a story.

Anyone with a basic command of the English language can write a story. The first story about John could have been written by a 3rd grader. But then, you'll remember that our goal is not just to write stories. We want to bring the reader into your mind, and help them understand who you are. The only thing we understand about John is that he's an obedient teenager.

In this book, you'll learn how to make a story engaging, by telling it in terms of experience, and not just observation. You'll learn how to organize it so that it flows from point to point without interruption. You'll learn how to make a story funny, and surprising.

So let's review. This book will teach you how to write a book. Specifically, it will teach you how to write stories so that others can get to know you (or your subject) better through it. And, it will teach you how to turn your stories into engaging experiences that can catch attention and hold your audience riveted until the last page. It's time to get to work.

PART 2

DISCOVERING YOUR STORY

Jason Lee

5

<u>Timeline</u>

I want you to think about your life. Think about the whole thing from your birth to the present day. What do you remember?

Chances are that you can't actually go back and live it all in your mind. There are probably little chunks that have faded from memory, and other things that you never even cared to remember. If you're like me, you might not even remember what you had for breakfast yesterday. Instead, you probably have some very specific memories that help you define who you are.

It's similar to the movie InsideOut. In the movie, the girl, Riley, has shelves and shelves of memories, but most of them are not constantly playing out. There are a few core memories that help her define who she is. There is also a massive number of memories that were simply forgotten.

The fact of the matter is that our brains weren't designed to keep all of our memories within easy reach. Instead, they get triggered when we see something that reminds us of them. Sometimes it's simple, like seeing a freezer full of ice cream and recalling that time that you had chocolate chunk ice cream and really enjoyed it. Sometimes they are more complex, like the emotional, traumatic experience of veterans dealing with triggers to their post traumatic stress disorder. But in both cases, the memories and consequences are triggered by something.

As a simple example of this, I want you to think of all the words you can remember. You can start by looking at the words in this sentence and moving on to the words that are similar to those. But, chances are that you wouldn't even think to use astrophysics terminology until being reminded of it by reading it just now. Memories work the same way, so to find the key memories that are going to make up your book, we are going to start by taking a stroll down memory lane, to see what we can dig up.

EXERCISE: A PERSONAL TIMELINE

Start by getting a sheet of paper. Depending on how old you are, or how good your memory is, you might want to get two. Turn the paper sideways so it's width is greater than its length. Now draw a line across the center from left to right. On the left edge of the line, write the word "BIRTH". On the right edge, write "NOW."

Make some tick marks to represent the major years at 10, 20, 30, etc.

Now, you are going to start to fill in the benchmarks in your life. Turn this paper into a timeline of your life. You don't have to go into terrible amounts of detail. We're not looking for full stories here. Just a little reminder. Write down the words and phrases that will help trigger the memories when you look back at them.

As you work through this exercise, I want you to go through the following questions one at a time. Each one is likely to trigger multiple memories, and that's just fine. The objective here is to get down as many of the little memories as we can. What is important is to not just write down names or dates, but think to specific things that happened with those people, or landmark moments on those dates.

- What memorable things happened in your childhood?

- Were there any major world events that happened? How did you react? How did things change?

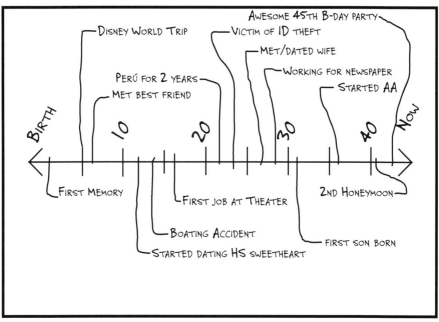

Like this example, you should fill up the page. Remember to focus on stories, and not just life events.

- Who was important in your childhood? Why?

- What stories do you remember about interacting with your parents, your siblings?

- Who are your best friends?

- When did you get married? What was it like when you were dating?

- What jobs did you have?

- Which jobs were better than others?

- What was your career?

- What fun things did you do with your friends?

- What decisions did you make that influenced the rest of your life?

- When did you have children?

- What stories can you remember about them when they were very young (i.e. that they might not remember)?

- What were your favorite experiences with your children?

- What events did you experience that changed the way you saw life?

- What was a time when you felt the most satisfied/happy? Why do you think you felt that way?

- What experiences taught you something valuable?

- What are your funniest moments?

Your goal should be to fill this paper up with memories and stories from your life. When you write down one event, think about what other events happened around it.

By the end, this paper should be very full. When you are done with the questions above, go back and read through everything you wrote down. Is there anything missing? The questions above are far from comprehensive, and you should put down anything that you think should be there.

If you are writing about someone who is already deceased, don't let that stop you from doing this exercise. You can do it for them, too, and will benefit from the exercise. If you don't know the answer to a question, that's ok! You probably don't know *anyone* as well as you know yourself. But, start with what you know, and go from there. You could even do some research into their life, and the events that happened near them to get an idea of their perspective.

Dearest reader, it's time to be blunt.

I have worked with enough people to know that chances are, you have just read through the bit above and "taken it in" with full intention to do it later, only to shrug it off. After all, reading the words I wrote are a lot easier than writing your own. I know because I have been one of those people. But, I'm actually going to ask you to pause.

Please understand that this exercise is the first step down the path. Take the time to really do this and make it work. It might take you a day or more to get it all down. You might want to ask your friends or family what stories they remember about you. Some people might get carried away with this and take a week or more. What I want you to read and understand right now is that creating your timeline is something for you to do, and not just read about doing. And, you know what the cool part about reading this book is? It's not going anywhere.

I promise not to leave or change the words in the time that it takes you to do your timeline. I also promise that doing it will change you, and bring you a new clarity in the process of writing. The rest of the book is going to make much more sense, and carry a whole new weight if you take the time to do this now.

So go ahead. Stick a bookmark here. Fold down the page on the dotted line so you know where you are, and then do the timeline. I'll be here.

Did it? Good.

Now that you're done, you have in your hands something that many people never get to see: a glimpse of a life. It's what you've been through, in a nutshell. But what is amazing about that sheet (or two) of paper in your hands is that it represents more knowledge about yourself than anyone else in the world knows about you, and that is saying something.

Did you know that Facebook can tell what your political leanings are, based on the links you click and the things you "like?" They can tell your religion, your voting tendencies, whether or not you tend to buy things with a credit or debit card, and even make a guess at your income. Scary, right? But, there are things that all of their data centers can't see.

They can't see the time you ran around your back yard, timing yourself to see how fast you could do it. They don't know what it was like to have the stopwatch in your hand.

They don't know what it felt like when you discovered your first crush, or the pure euphoria you experienced when you actually got to spend time with them.

They can't understand why you and your best friend from high school still crack up when you whisper certain phrases to each other.

We have the tendency to see ourselves in terms of labels. Gay or straight. Conservative or Liberal. Religious or atheist. We tend to look at those simple words as who we are, and forget the stories that made the label stick. As you sit there looking over your timeline, can you see the flow of your life? Can you see the points where things changed?

This book isn't meant to be a self help/personal development book, but you might want to take a moment to really reflect over your life in this moment when you can see it. What lessons can you see in your life that you might not have noticed without this bird's eye view? What were your failings? What are your strengths? How could you teach these lessons to others?

This exercise will not only give you a small succinct view of your life to consult while writing, it will also give you a big picture view to help see the turning points that made you into who you are, and define what you stand for.

If you are writing about someone else, then this timeline can be even more insightful. What kind of connections can you see now? What decisions made the difference for them?

6

<u>W</u>RITING <u>O</u>NE-ON-<u>O</u>NE

There is a significant temptation when writing to think that writing is about you. Especially when you are writing something as significant as a personal history, you might want to think that you are writing to "tell your story." Let me give you a quick hint right here at the beginning:

Your story is not worth anything without a *reader*.

If your story doesn't get read, or isn't meant for anyone, it is like the metaphorical tree falling in the forest with no one around. The debate is too often about whether or not the tree makes a sound. The truth is that it doesn't matter whether it does or not. If Shakespeare's best work was actually lost before anyone could read it, we might include references to it in anthologies, but it would never receive the applause of the crowd, or change the world.

What this means for you is that as you look through your timeline, I want you to think about the people who you want to read your book. And, I don't mean in a collective general audience way either.

I mean in a personal, one-on-one sort of way. Imagine that you are in a hospital on your deathbed and someone you care about happens to walk in the door. What would you tell them? Your writing should be the same way.

I'm not saying that it should be laced with references to "when I'm gone" or "take advantage of the time with me while you can." Your book should be honest in that way that death seems to provoke. As you write, look to be open and to help someone, and not just spout off about something that happened.

EXERCISE: SIGNIFICANT OTHERS

First, get out another blank sheet of paper. Now, as you look over your timeline, think about who you wish could know you better. Who needs to know the lessons you've learned?

Write down one name at the top of the blank sheet. Choose the most important one. Someone who you want to really connect with.

Underneath their name, write down the names of the stories you want to tell them. Again, you don't have to write out the whole story now. Just use a few key words to remind you which story it was.

Write down a new name under that and repeat with stories the new person needs to hear. Do this as many times as you think you need to.

As you work your way down the sheet of paper, think about the individual people that you want to tell the stories to. Think about the lessons you have learned throughout your life.

Even if you have told them the story a hundred times before, how could you change a life with one more telling? The stories you tell to the ones you love will stay with them for a lifetime, and repetition will help them to remember them more clearly.

NAME	STORY
My Sons	How Dungeons and Dragons changed my life
	Dealing with an Internet full of Porn
	Learning to date with My HS sweetheart
My Grandchildren	What my religion meant to me (using church camp story)
	The satisfaction at a good day's work (first job)
My Wife	Growing up with a friend with Autism
	Why I love to read (Mom teaching me how)

As you think about the people you are writing to, consider this: What things might you have experienced that they might not have? What lessons did you learn from the major world events from previous decades?

Later, when you start to actually write your stories down, think about these people as you write them. Make your stories as if you were writing to them specifically. If you do, you'll find that your book will feel less like a text book, and more like a heartfelt letter. It's worth asking:

Which would you rather read?

7

TURNING POINTS

Many of the most significant stories tell what happened at "turning points" either in your life or in the world around you. Have you ever wondered why all good romantic comedies start at the end of one relationship and the beginning of one that is obviously "so much better?" It's because we are suckers for a good turning point.

A story about a turning point essentially says, 'things were different after *this* happened.' It might be for better or for worse, but you know that your life will never be the same. You like those movies and books. We all do. Depending on how strongly the story stirred your emotions, you might even say that the book or movie "changed your life."

Wait... Think about that for just a second.

You spent a few hours staring at ink on a page, or actors on a screen, and were so affected by the story you saw that you might actually *live your life differently* because of it.

This is because of an amazing act of neuroscience. When you hear a story, your brain releases a chemical called oxytocin. This simple molecule causes your brain to light up in about the same way as the story teller's brain did. It puts you in sync with them. Have you ever felt yourself crying during a sad movie? Maybe you got tense during a scene in a drama. Or maybe, you just felt inspired by the end of the story. That means that you and everyone in the room with you likely felt something similar. Your bodies were each releasing the same chemicals, and going through a similar process. Your emotions were influenced in a similar way. In other words, a good story makes your body release a chemical that helps you relate.

What this means is that by sharing the stories that made a difference in your life, you can make a difference in the life of someone else. How amazing is that? Did it ever occur to you that all of history is passed down from one generation to the next with stories? Maybe our civilization advances only according to the stories we tell each other, the turning points we learn as a community. What you need to ask yourself is, what are those turning points in my life?

I'll give you some hints. For most people, there are some pretty big ones that change everything for them. They are pretty common life experiences that most of us will go through, but knowing that we will go through them doesn't change the fact that we learn lessons that can help others. For example, what did you learn from the following events in your own life:

- Getting Married
- Having sex for the first time (gasp!)
- Your first breakup
- The birth of your first child
- The death of someone close to you (parent, child, sibling, or friend)

Each of these is a near universal experience, which means two things. First, whoever you are writing to will almost undoubtedly have either experienced them or will experience them in the future. And second, a description of your experience will show them how you thought about and dealt with it. Seeing things from your perspective on the event can be an extremely powerful tool in opening their eyes.

You have your own personal turning points as well. Maybe you had a close encounter with death when you were a father or mother. How did that affect the way you saw or treated your children? Maybe you had a moment where your belief system became more solid, or a moment where it changed entirely. What did that process look like? What did it mean to the way that you lived your life? In the end, this is what a turning point boils down to: An event that changed the way you live.

Also, there are turning points in world history where everything changes. I have a little brother who is significantly younger than I am. Where most of us can remember exactly where we were when the twin towers of the World Trade Center fell on September 11, 2001, he wasn't even a year old at the time. He has grown up in a post 9/11 world, where terrorism is a buzz word that gets thrown about by pundits on a daily basis. I have a perspective from that world that existed before, that he can't know without our stories. He knows about it in theory, but doesn't really doesn't know what the difference *feels like*. How else can he know without a story?

There have been big events in every decade that have changed the way that the world works, creating turning points that you can provide your insight on. If you can't think of any, try these big landmarks:

- 1950's - The beginning of the Cold War
- 1960's - The Sexual Revolution
- 1970's - The Vietnam War
- 1980's - End of the Soviet Union and fall of the Berlin Wall
- 1990's - The beginning of the internet
- 2000's - 9/11 and the beginning of the War on Terrorism

These are just some of the big ones. I'm sure you can think of more historical turning points. Which ones were significant for you, or the people you want to write about? If you go back in history, which events impacted the lives of our ancestors?

EXERCISE: BEFORE AND AFTER

Once again, go and get out blank sheet of paper. Make three columns down the center of the paper. In the first

BEFORE	STORY	AFTER
BUSH v GORE AMERICA IS THE BEST	9/11	TERRORISM HOMELAND DEFENSE
PARENTS WERE GOOD FOR RETIREMENT	2008 CRASH	I HAD TO PUT MYSELF THROUGH COLLEGE
PRESIDENTS ARE ALL GOOD PEOPLE	PRESIDENT CLINTON SCANDAL	OFFICE DOES NOT GUARANTEE GOODNESS

column, write the word *Before*. In the second, write the word *Story*, and in the third, write the word *After*. Think about the turning points you've had in your life, personal, universal, or other. For each one, write down what life was like for you both before and after the turning point story. Can you see how that one turning point made a difference?

Feel free to use this exercise with stories you already have listed from other exercises to help you see their impact. Using this exercise can help create a more in-depth view of your family's history as well. Using these turning points can help to flesh out a life that might otherwise be rather blank. You'll also find that you can connect more with others by thinking about what turning points they have lived through.

These turning points help make a life real, and feel like someone actually lived through it. Using these stories can turn a list of facts into a veritable time machine to see what life was actually like.

8

Choosing Stories: The Funnel

So now you've created a timeline. You've looked at the people you want to write to. And, you've looked at the turning points that have been critical to the way you live your life. My guess is that you have a lot of ideas about stories to write.

As cool as it might be to eventually write down all of those stories, we need to narrow things down a little bit. Memoirs are powerful when they touch on a few specific stories that are the most impactful or the most revealing. Even good biographies have to pick and choose the stories that they are going to tell.

Our goal now is to pick the stories that must be told, and leave the rest alone for a while. If your book is a hit, and begs for a sequel, then you'll have more to draw on later, but for now, let's get the first round.

For this step, let's look to write around ten stories in your first book.

I know. You're probably looking at your different sheets and thinking, "But I have so many more!" And that's great! It means that you have material for a second book. But for this first one, we really want to focus on a few great stories that are going to paint a clear picture.

There's a reason I choose the number ten. Many people think about writing a history of anything and get overwhelmed. It seems like too much, or they question where to begin. But by narrowing it down, it gives you a specific goal. You can write down, and work on ten good, life-changing stories, right? Then let's figure out which ones those are.

EXERCISE: THE FUNNEL

By this point, you should have three sheets of paper from the exercises in the previous chapters. You should have a timeline, a list of people you want to tell stories to, and a list of turning points in your life. The first step in figuring out which stories to tell is to look at all three and look for the stories they have in common. Circle these stories, or make a separate list of them.

Which stories are on each list? Are there stories that hit all three? Chances are these are the important ones. They figure into your timeline, would mean a lot to the right person, and are a turning point in your own life. Each of these stories has the potential to make it into your memoirs.

If you do not have your ten stories yet, then check the stories that are in common between the Significant Others sheet and your Turning Points sheet. Add these stories to your list.

To bring down the number of stories you have (if you have more than ten), take the stories you have and list them in order of importance to you. Your goal is to take the top ten, and then keep the rest on hold for a later date. If you are having a hard time cutting back, it is ok to go as high as 13, but remember that this is going to be a lot of work, and we don't really want to add more on top of it if we can help it.

Once you have decided on your top ten stories to write out, put your other sheets in a safe place. They are still very valuable, and could be a great resource if you decide to write another book.

What is more, those sheets of paper, especially your timeline, could end up in your book to show just how much more you did with your life. You don't have to have all of the details for people to know what happened to you. It's just fine to share that you were on your honeymoon in the Carribean without sharing what happened.

When you're done, let's move on to the next section, the one where we start to really make your stories come to life. It's time to learn to write.

PART 3

LEARNING TO WRITE

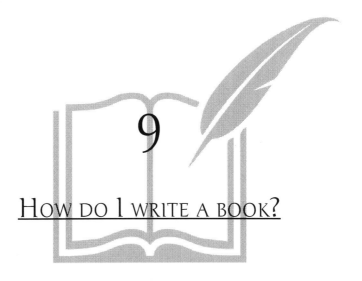

9

HOW DO I WRITE A BOOK?

That's a great question. After all, there are hundreds of new books being published every day. Some estimates even place the number as high as 5,000 books every day.

That's a lot of books.

So before we get too far into this, there is one thing that you should know: chances are, your book will not sell well. In fact, the chances of you making any real amount of money through writing your memoirs and publishing them is incredibly small. But then, if you are writing memoirs to get money to retire on, you are probably in the wrong profession.

Professional authors spend years marketing their books and getting agents and publishers to put their books in the right places so people will buy them and read them. It takes lots of perseverance and wading through rejection after rejection. I won't say that it's impossible, but I also didn't write this book to teach you how to do that. So let's be clear on this point from the very beginning:

I am not teaching you to make money by becoming a professional author. I am teaching you to write stories that matter in a way people will read.

Second, as much as we would all like to be famous, writing your memoirs probably won't do that either. I'm not in the business of teaching you how to write like an award-winning author. But, that's ok. You don't need to be a super witty, amazing writer to be worth reading. My goal is to help you write something that is worth reading. I'm going to teach you some simple tricks that will elevate your writing to the next level, and help your readers enjoy your book. I'm going to help you use your stories to connect.

The act of writing a book does not mean that everyone is going to read it. In fact, you will have to talk to people and convince them to read it. If your writing is completely unintelligible, or just straight up boring, you are going to have a much harder time of doing that. Reaching a wider audience requires marketing, publishers, and agents, and like I mentioned before, I'm not going to teach you to do that. But before you get all of that, you need to have a book that is *readable* and at least mildly entertaining.

This sounds hard. Why should I learn how to write again?

Actually, the tricks I'm going to teach you are relatively simple. If you want to learn how to become a professional author, then get ready for a hard time. Your history is about something much more than a number in your bank account, or a fifteen minute TV spot with Oprah. A personal or family history is about who you are.

When you look back at the past, there is a lot of history to see. You can see the great pyramids at Giza, or the Parthenon in Greece. But, as amazing as they are, the things we actually know about those people comes because of *writing*.

Did you know that we have accounting records from ancient Sumeria from 4000 BC? Rather than guess what these people actually traded and did, we have records to rely on. Many people revere Greek culture as the birthplace of what we now consider "Western" thought, but that conception really only exists because we have writing from the people who lived there. The names of Plato and Aristotle are known because of their writing.

> *"Either write something worth reading, or do something worth writing."*
> *-Benjamin Franklin*

But, what if you're not the 21st century's equivalent of Aristotle. Should you still write? In my mind, it has always come down to one simple question: Will you tell me a story?

Note that I didn't ask if you had a world-altering story, or a story that everyone finds fascinating. All it takes is a story. And any story will do.

You see, for thousands of years, knowing how to read and write was a mystery to all but the select few at the top of the food chain. It wasn't common. And so the stories of the world were dictated by those few who could write them. But for the others, their lives have all but disappeared.

I have an ancestor whose life can be summed up with two numbers: one that says when he was born, and another that says when he died.

Those numbers don't say where he were born, or how. They don't say whether or not his parents were in love, or just doing what society expected of them. I don't know how much money he had growing up, or who his friends were, or whether or not he was happy. I don't know his story. What I know about his life is summed up by the dash in between two year markers.

His life was essentially erased from history, simply because no one told his story.

On the other hand, I have another ancestor named William Lee who immigrated from Ireland to the Colonies in 1745. He fought in the Revolutionary War, and lost a leg in the battle for Guilford County Courthouse in the Carolinas William was left for dead on the battlefield. A nurse stumbled upon him and took care of him until he was healthy. Through the whole ordeal, they fell in love and were married, eventually having four children. I am descended from his youngest son, Samuel.

This simple story, while far from a complete biography, paints a picture of resilience and determination. His blood flows through my veins, and I can feel echoes of his story in my own. I am better for it.

What if I don't want to be the one to write it?

In writing your book, you have the opportunity to do something much greater than make a little money, or get a spot on daytime TV. You can leave your mark on the history of the world. You have the amazing opportunity to introduce yourself to generations to come, and reintroduce yourself to the people that matter most in your life.

I don't care if you think that you've never done anything significant in the hundred years you've been alive. You have a story, and if you don't tell it, it will die with you.

Luckily for you, though, you don't necessarily have to be the one who writes it down. The next few chapters are going to be on writing and improving your own writing. However, there is actually a short cut that a lot of people take.

It's called a ghostwriter. A ghostwriter is someone who will talk with you and get to know your story and write it for you. They'll write under your name and you'll still get the credit for it. You just pay them a fee to write for you. I actually work as one, and can say that the experience is incredible. It's one of the big reasons why I am so passionate about people writing their stories. If I'm being honest, I don't even care if someone pays me to write their story for them or not, *as long as it gets told.*

This is because the wheels of history turn on small decisions, and your decisions may just echo for generations to come. We progress as a human race because we learn from those that come before us, and your memoirs, your memories, your stories are a part of that.

You can't know when your struggles and problems will provide just the solution that someone else needs. Your son might just need to know that he's not alone in trying to provide for a young family. Your spouse might be waiting to see you through new eyes, and fall in love again. Your great great grandson might need a story of encouragement from a time when things were much rougher than they will be in his day. Your words might never reach the New York Times Bestseller list, but never underestimate the difference they can make in the world.

I wrote this book to urge you to write your own, and to teach you how to do it. The writing is not hard, and will make all the difference to those to come.

10

THE B.U.D.

Every beautiful flower starts as a bud. Buds aren't particularly beautiful, and they're definitely not finished flowers. But, those flowers have to start somewhere.

Every beautiful book starts as a B.U.D., too: a Big Ugly Draft. They're not pretty, but that's because, like a good flower bud, they're not quite done growing yet.

Most of the time, people write something up, and then call it good. They send it off, or click post, or send, and never even stop to read it twice. Judging by some of the stuff I've read, it looks like some people don't think about it very much the first time they're writing it, either.

This leads to problems. When you're content with the first thing that drops out of your brain, there are errors. We don't write exactly what we mean. If we're lucky, those mistakes are just confusing or distracting. If you're not so fortunate, they could end up like this year book picture where the parents were so proud of their son's baseball career. But, trust me when I say that no one wants to be remembered as a Home Run "Hitler."

Congrats to our Home Run Hitler. Class of 2013 Love Mom, Dad, and Kota

Now, with all of that said, you have to start somewhere, and for that first time around, it's ok to make the mistake of referring to your son as Hitler.

That's because the first time around, the most important part of it all is getting it down. Once you have the basic pieces down, you can start to play with what you've actually written, and make it better. It will be later on that you correct everything and dethrone your son as the leader of the Nazi regime. And, you don't need to remember every detail of every story. Right now, all you need to write is a B.U.D.

In fact, we want a certain mindset from the onset. Your first draft is going to be big and ugly, and that is *great*. That's because it's not the final draft, and you're free to make some mistakes. After all, this is just one of a few drafts. It's a try, a first pass, a single attempt.

That means you sit down and write it out. It can be ugly and totally disheveled and no one will care. In fact, the whole reason that you're doing it is so that you have something you can eventually make really good. But, first things first.

You've chosen ten stories to become your ten chapters. Now, let's put them to writing. Part of the reason why I went through the whole editing thing first so that you keep something in mind while you are writing your draft. It will be Big and Ugly. To reiterate: *that's okay.*

> *"The scariest part is always just before you start."*
>
> *-Stephen King*

It is way more important at this point to get the story and words down than for it to be wonderful. Many people will claim that they want to write a book, only to get caught up before they even begin the process. Athena, the Greek goddess, sprang fully formed from Zeus's head. Please understand that she is the exception and not the rule.

So what is the best way to actually go about this? I recommend one of two methods for writing a draft:

1)   The blank page.

Start with a blank page, whether it is physical or digital. I tend to use digital because it tends to be easier to edit afterwards, but it is by no means necessary. Next, set aside the time and commit to staying there until you have written the story down. Then you start writing.

Remember, it doesn't have to be perfect. You just have to get it down. The important part of this method is the commitment to stay put. You will get distracted. You will think that you should wait till later. Don't get up until the story is down. When you get stumped about how to say something, just write down the garbled words in your head. When you lose the creative urge, keep writing. This B.U.D. *will* eventually grow into that pretty flower you want, but it has to start somewhere.

2) The time limit.

Set yourself a very tight deadline. For a single story, I would recommend no longer than an hour. Then, force yourself to get the whole story out in that time limit. Just like the blank page, your goal is not perfection.

The whole point of the time limit is to put some pressure on you to get it done. The idea is to trick your brain into getting the story out on paper where you can begin to tweak it and turn it into what you actually want.

With both of these methods, the challenge is actually starting. There are a hundred different reasons why you should put off writing until tomorrow, or next month. I'm going to call each of those reasons out for what they are:

Excuses.

Everyone of them is an excuse born of fear. You can wallow in it, and tell yourself that you're just waiting for [insert excuse here], or you can suck it up and get on with it.

When you think about the book you are going to write,

it is easy to get excited about the end product. But the actual process is much more exciting than fantasizing about a finished product. So my challenge to you is to *set a date*. Right now, before you go on to the next chapter, set a date and time when you will begin work on your BUD. Set that time for a day within the next week. I didn't write this book to teach you a nice theoretical method to write a book at some point in your life. I want you to start now. Write that date on the line below, and commit to it.

I also want to you keep on reading. Even though your BUD won't be completed yet, I want you to read ahead so that you know what is coming. Mostly because the next few chapters will give you some ideas as you write out your BUD. They'll introduce some spice into your writing process and help your writing become a little bit better.

I, _____ WILL BEGIN TO WRITE DOWN MY STORIES INTO A BIG UGLY DRAFT ON

_____.

SIGNED: _____

11

<u>Show, Don't tell.</u>

If you've been in a 6th grade writing class, you've probably heard the phrase, "Show, don't tell." It seems to be one of the staples of writing. You have to "show" the reader what you mean, instead of just "telling" them. Simple, right?

Not usually. This becomes doubly true if you are telling an ancestor's story instead of just your own.

Unfortunately, this particular phrase doesn't explain much in the way of how to actually create that sort of writing. You would probably know if an author had shown you something instead of told you it, but that doesn't mean that you innately know how to do it yourself.

Instead, I'm going to teach you how to do this. Let me give you an example exercise. Here is your phrase:

There is an apple in my hand.

I have just told you something. Now we are going to take this "telling" and turn it into "showing."

You might be looking at this thinking, Jason, that doesn't make any sense. What more is there to show? Or, you might have a bunch of writing on a page that looks something like this:

I could feel the round fruit pressing down gently onto my palm, its weight familiar to me. The shiny, polished skin tenderly nestled itself against my curled fingertips. Against the florescent light, the bright red blush coalesced to the top, where it tucked into the ruddy, browned stem that protruded from it, like a clipped, herbaceous umbilical cord.

The second example is a little different, right?

While exaggerated, the second is undeniably more fun to read. So here's the million dollar question: How do you go from one to the other? How do you actually write a description that is "showing" and not just "telling?"

There are three levels to making this work. Each one is crucial to taking your story from a set of facts to a powerful story. Yet, each one works a little differently. So pay attention, and we'll start at level one.

LEVEL ONE: COMMON SENSE.

This first level is the easiest to look for. If you are describing an apple, go through the five senses.

> *"Don't tell me the moon is shining; show me the glint of light on broken glass"*
>
> *-Anton Chekhov*

- What does it look like?
- What does it sound like?
- What does it feel like?
- What does it smell like?
- What does it taste like?

Simple, right? So instead of the word apple, you now have a set of descriptions that can "show" what an apple is. It's not just an apple in your hand. It's a red, smooth, fragrant, sweet fruit that makes a thud when it falls to the ground. But that's just the beginning of using your senses.

You see, we connect sense with memory, so instead of writing, *the fruit was red,* you can compare it to something else that is red. You could write, the apple was as red as a stop sign.

I know this all seems simplistic now, but when you apply it to your stories, they are going to become significantly better. You might not have any apples in your stories, but you'll find that this technique works well in any environment. For example:

We sloshed through mud that was about as fragrant as a baby's diaper.

Simple, but effective.

You can use this all over the place to add depth to your writing and to make it more interesting. Just this one simple technique will add all kinds of interesting bits to your book. But that's just the beginning...

LEVEL TWO: GETTING ALL EMOTIONAL.

So level one was about the senses. Taste, sight, smell, touch, sound. The next level, though, is about something deeper: emotion.

When you add emotional words to your description of events, you radically change the way that your reader experiences them. And, the cool part is that it doesn't even take that many words. Watch this:

I held the rosy little apple in my hand and felt its cool, refreshing skin.

Sounds like a really good apple, right? You feel affection for it. When I write, "rosy little" it brings to mind something that is cute, something that you like. And the skin wasn't slightly chilled. It was cool and refreshing, bringing to mind the emotion of relief after the sun.

By putting in a few words, the apple becomes our friend. Can it work the other way? Of course. Watch this:

The apple fell heavily into my hand, its sickeningly sweet aroma penetrating my nostrils.

This time, the apple "fell heavily" as if there were some unwanted outcome attached to it. And that "sickeningly sweet aroma?" It creates a feeling of disgust. And we won't even go into the idea of penetrating.

So was it the same apple? It could have been. But, the description of each leads us to feel very differently about them. You were shown very different sides of that apple. One was delightful, and friendly. The other was ominous and abusive.

Putting emotion into a description is about looking beyond the actual events that you are describing. It's about remembering the emotions that you felt, and helping your reader to feel the same.

For example, did you ever have a time when you disliked your boss? Instead of just saying that you "loathe" your boss, write that loathing into his description:

> *The mean little man always exited his office with a smirk. It was like he had looked around the room and loved that he got to lord himself over it. And, if you watched him long enough, you could see him constantly pushing up the glasses that had slipped while looking down at you over his nose through them.*

You don't need to say that you loathed the man. Because of your description, we already feel the same way.

So how do you make this happen? Well, to start out, I'm going to use a word that you might find offensive. It's the "E" word. That's right. You should exaggerate.

But, isn't that lying?

Well, yes and no. This book you're writing is about you. That means that it's about your perspective, your experience, and your emotions. You can even put a little disclaimer into your introduction saying as much. As long as the story accurately reflects your memory, and conveys that to your reader, you are being honest. In fact, describing things through what feels like exaggerated emotion is likely more true than your perfect hindsight tells you. This is significantly more honest than if you had just said that you didn't like your boss.

Wait a second, I hear you say. It sounded like you just said that it was more accurate to lie. That sounds like a justification for dishonesty.

No. Let me be clear first off and say that I do not condone dishonesty, and that kind of creative license is not the type you should take in your own memoirs. You don't need to lie to impress people here. What I'm teaching you to do is take advantage of something our brains do to help us remember things better. It's called emotional filtering, and we use it all the time, whether we realize it or not.

Emotional filtering is the process whereby your brain attaches emotion to a memory in order to better remember it in the future.

Remember at the beginning of this chapter where I told you that I had an apple in my hand? You probably remember it vaguely. It has become a triggered memory: something you remember because I mentioned it, and not because you have any real care about that original sentence. But if I asked you to recall the emotions associated with that apple when I wrote about it most recently, can you remember them? Chances are, those memories come back much clearer.

This is because your mind uses emotion as an emphasis for memory. If someone's dad got drunk when they were a child and had the tendency to get violent, then chances are they remember being scared. That entire memory is vivid because it is colored by the terror that he would turn on them. It stands out from everyday life as a child.

When describing a memory like that, you might be tempted to shy away from the emotion, or think that it's private. I don't blame you if you want to keep your emotions to yourself. Sharing them feels vulnerable and feels like you are inviting ridicule. But, if there is one thing that I've learned about writing, it's that people want you to be open with them. A book where you state what happened might give an "accurate" account of the events, but a book where you help your reader experience your emotions will reach out and touch them in ways that they weren't expecting. And that actually leads us to level three, experience.

LEVEL THREE: RE-LIVING YOUR MEMORY.

There is a power in your memories. It is the power of your character, shining back at you through the years. And, the way that you show that to someone is to take them there. When you are writing your memory as a window to your own past, it takes on a life of its own. It becomes something more than words on a page.

It takes descriptions and emotions and rolls them all up into a giant ball called experience, where the reader becomes you for a brief moment in time. They experience what you experience.

The reader is no longer reading about an apple. He is remembering a specific apple, and the time that he held it.

Your reader experiences:

I reached into the wooden bowl and found the apple. My fingers wrapped around it and brought it out so I could look at it for a moment. The red skin shined in the lights of the kitchen, reflecting back at me. I rubbed the apple on my shirt to clean it. It was a habit that I had maintained since childhood, even though I'm still not sure whether or not it actually does anything. Finally, I brought the fruit to my mouth and felt the slight hesitation as my teeth punctured the outer skin and sunk into the sweet, yet tart, white flesh. I wanted to enjoy the rest of it, but at a call from the other room I left the apple on the table to rush to see what was wrong. I never finished that apple...

Experiences, like the example above, do not simply start or end in a vacuum. They arrive in context. You do not wake up in the morning, have a spectacular day, and then go back to business as usual the next day. There is anticipation, or surprise proceeding the day. Following it is a slow settle back into the routine, or maybe the setting of new routines.

In writing your memoirs, you'll be picking out specific memories to share. But, none of those stories will occur in a vacuum. Each one can give a glimpse into your mind and life during that time period.

So how do you do it? How do you write an experience? You put your story in context. Don't just write:

It was February 25th, 1984.

That string of numbers means almost nothing to the human mind without finding a reference point. Instead, write:

I remember a day back in 1984, not too long after Ronald Reagan said he was going for reelection.

If you don't remember what was going on in the world, look it up! There are some great internet resources for finding historical events based on dates. If you don't care about the exact date, consider working in some descriptions that help place the time period, or the place where you were living. For example:

I was sitting one day in my old rocking chair, rubbing my bare feet on our olive green shag carpet.

There's not even a year, but the carpet gives the impression of the 60's or 70's. There are hundreds of ways you can put your story in context. One great way to go about it is to ask the question: what things did I take for granted? Answers to this question will give you your setting, and provide the context you are looking for.

So what do you get when you combine all three levels of "showing" instead of telling? You end up with a story that feels real, and not just like a collection of facts.

IMPORTANT NOTE:

If you are writing about someone else's experience, you might think that you can't get that detailed with the stories. This is utterly false! Use the internet to look up conditions during those times. Read their journals to glean details you might have missed before. Most importantly, use your imagination! None of us is so different that we can't figure out what it might have been like to live through another's stories. A big part of making these stories powerful is not just in the descriptions, but in how we tell them, and which parts we emphasize. The next chapter will help you do just that.

12

TAKING YOUR STORY APART.

Writing a story these days is not nearly as straightforward as you might think. It requires more than just saying what happened, and good stories are *engineered* to make an impact. Luckily, the techniques that are used are not difficult to learn, and can be fun to play with.

Some are really simple, like the Dramatic Reveal. To do a Dramatic Reveal, all you need to do is tell your story normally, from start to finish, but leave out one crucial part, the "punchline" if you will. It might be a story about the time you met someone on the bus and decided to go on an impromptu date and ended up having a really nice time. Even though the relationship never went anywhere, you'll always remember that amazing day that you had with Robin Williams, or Celine Dion. By leaving out that one little bit of information, you set up a climax that is sure to turn heads.

Others take a little more thought to pull off. That's why this chapter and the next few chapters are going to focus, not on how to write a story, but on the different pieces of your story.

When young people are taught how to write a story, they are usually given a diagram like this one:

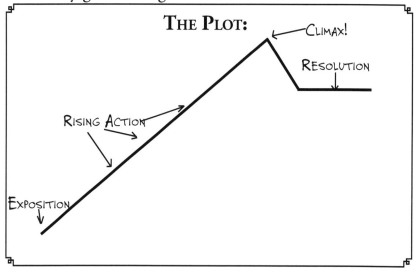

It's quaint and shows a nice little path to follow. You start with the Exposition, which is really just a fancy name for the setting. Then, you have rising action, the things that happen before the climax. The climax is the big exciting outcome. It's where all the tension finally explodes. Then the action calms down from there until you find the resolution, the end place.

If that's how you want your story to be, then go for it. You can definitely do a story this way. But, in a memoir, things get kind of interesting. The rules don't always get followed. Instead of one story, memoirs have lots of them. Each story is something small, some tiny part of the whole. And, there is a very good reason for this: lives don't follow the story plot.

We are born, and immediately start having different ups and downs. Some days we nap and smile. Other days we sit in a stinky diaper. I know that you have had good weeks and bad weeks. Some of them are even significant enough to become memories that you carry with you. They become the stories that you use to define who you are. But, in the course of your life, can you honestly identify the "climax" of your life? Was everything previous to it just "rising action?" And, at what time did your life suddenly just "resolve?" If life were that straight forward, every life would be a movie.

It's a little difficult, and not particularly true to shove your story into the plot diagram. Instead, I want you to look at each of your stories in terms of three pieces: Setting, Climax, and Moral.

Yes, you will have more to the story than these, but by identifying these pieces, you will be able to play with and enjoy your stories, and tell them in new and exciting ways. For example, the traditional view says that you tell the setting first and then build to the climax. Afterwards, you get to the resolution where you can tell the moral. This is just how stories go, right? Let's play with an example story from my own childhood:

The week before I started kindergarten, my mom introduced me to a boy who would become my best friend through elementary school. His name was Brendan Canfield, and he had Asperger's Syndrome. Today, we simply refer to these people as being high functioning autistic, but the label wouldn't have changed the way that elementary school played out for him.

He was always a little weird, and little slow, but he was genuine and honest to a fault. To me, he was a good person at heart, and he deserved a chance. Unfortunately, that chance was not often granted by the unforgiving kids

that we went to school with. It became a game to ask him questions that he didn't know the answer to, and then laugh as he gave the best answer he could.

I don't know when I made the decision to stand by him. Maybe it was when my mom told me to be his friend. Maybe it was when I saw that he needed one. Either way, we became friends, and I decided to stand up for him, despite his learning disabilities and awkwardness.

We did everything together for years until the end of 6th grade. I was at home when I overheard my mom talking with his about them moving away. I wasn't sure what to do. It sounded pretty insubstantial at the time, and I did what most kids my age would have done: I ignored it and hoped for the best.

But, time passed, and that insubstantial conversation became more and more concrete until Brendan and I were left to count the days.

And then, he was gone.

I wasn't sure what I would do. I didn't know who I was without him. I had spent so many years with him that to have my best friend move away was just painful, and confusing. I would ride my bike by his house and see the unfamiliar faces, and wonder, time and time again, what I had lost.

Years later, I realized that while the friend had left my life, there were some things that he had left behind. I had learned to stand up for people who no one else would give a second glance to. I learned to ignore the stares and the ridicule. I had learned what it meant to be a hero.

It's a good story, right? It has each of the three pieces: Setting, Climax, and Moral. The order is great. It follows that chart from earlier and creates the perfect plot. Good to go, right?

But, what if we tried something different? What if we mixed up the order a little bit? For example, what would happen to the story if we started right at the climax? Would it ruin the story? Let's find out:

Everyday, I rode my bike by the house and saw the new, unfamiliar faces in it, and wondered what exactly I had lost. Who was I, now that he didn't live there anymore? Why couldn't I fit together the pieces? Where were the fun, relaxed days I had spent with my best friend just last summer?

Not quite eight years earlier, I was sitting in a classroom when my mom came in and introduced me to a quiet boy named Brendan Canfield, who would become my best friend...

You can see how it would go from there. The story still

plays out, but the climax, *the climax*, is right there at the beginning! It acts like a hook and begs the reader to find out how we got there. And we could keep mixing it up. We could start out with the moral and go from there:

> *Sometimes, people come into your life and teach you a lesson more valuable than anything you could possibly do for them. For me, that person was a boy named Brendan Canfield, who taught me, without words, how to be a hero. He didn't do it with a spectacular example of heroic deeds, or even with a show of great leadership. He did it by being a young boy who needed a friend, and someone to stand up for him.*

I started by telling the moral of the story first. There's now room to transition into the setting and the climax, all the while giving the reader something to look for: a lesson in heroism.

Mixing up and playing with the order of the pieces is one of the best tools that authors use to create stories that feel real and engage with their readers. In the next few chapters, I'm going to go over just what makes a good Setting, Moral, and Climax so that you can begin your own masterpieces to fill your book.

13

THE SETTING:
GIVING THE RIGHT CONTEXT.

When you're writing your book, you will want to spend a lot of time on this section. You could write an entire chapter just on the setting of your life. People do. In fact, the further back you go in time, the more necessary this part is.

Why?

Because it gives the context for the climax. Your stories don't take place in a vacuum, and often, the little pieces are what make all the difference. Leaving out the wrong pieces of your setting as you work towards the climax is kind of like forgetting to tell part of the joke before you get to the punchline. They might understand what is going on, but the impact is lost as they sort out the details.

Each story is going to need a little bit of setting. It might be as simple as stating that one story took place later in the year from the proceeding story. Or, there might be years in between stories. Either way, your stories will need to be set in time.

So what pieces are necessary for a good setting? Things that are different from today. What types of things does that actually mean? Let's get into it a little bit.

Date

The first thing you need to look at is the date of your story. You don't have to be exact, but by placing it in a bracket of time, you at least give a basic frame of reference. For example, did this particular story take place in the early 80's? by putting this little label in there, you evoke a time period that others can relate to. Even if they can't, a time frame gives your reader a set of preconceived notions that they can rely on to give context. This doesn't mean that you're done, but it does give you and your reader a starting point. You might not even end up writing the date, but by having this in your mind, it will help you get the next context pieces right.

Technology

What technology is mentioned in your story? Cell phones? Car phones? Cars? Look at the differences between how things are today and how they were in your story. Did talking on the phone mean that it had a curly cord that attached it to the wall? Were you able to check something on the internet, or did you have to go to the library to research a topic? This is the section that will probably make you feel the most old. However, you don't need to spell out every little difference between today and then, just the ones that might confuse your reader, or that are significant to your story. Work on being succinct here: clear, but short.

Politics

Politics isn't just about who's president. It refers to relationships and the way people interact. What relationships are mentioned in your story? Can you remember the first black people to go to your school? Explain that it was a new thing and that tensions were high. How were relations with Russia/China/the Middle East? It is okay to mention some social tension coming from the unknown. On the other hand, it might be as simple as saying that you and your Dad didn't always see eye to eye, especially where girls were involved. Put in a few words to give your reader a background on the relationships you will be talking about.

Location

Places change over time. I can remember when the hill on the way to my school was home to groundhogs instead of condos. I can also remember when they gassed them all. Putting in little details like how the places have changed gives a sense of connection to the past, even if you don't start it off with, "Back in *my* day..." These little anecdotes aren't the focus of the story, but they breathe life into it. Showing how places evolve over time can help your reader feel the passage of time, and see how they fit into the story.

Setting things up

In each of these examples, the important piece to note is that the setting describes how things *were*. If they've changed or if everyone's experience is different, your setting helps clarify and set up the story for the climax.

At this point, I could go into all of the rising action stuff that the charts seem to think is so important. But, all of the action in a story, no matter how long it is, is there for one reason. It's there to set up the climax.

In Tolkien's masterwork, The Lord of the Rings, there is a lot of setting. He was the first truly great fantasy author to establish an entire world where his story took place. Those who read it are submitted to extensive descriptions of the weather, the mythology, the languages, the songs, and the history of the world. There are those who argue that there is *too much* setting in Lord of the Rings. They want more action, drama, and story. So in comes Peter Jackson, the director of the new movies from the same franchise.

People love them. His movies make Lord of the Rings into mainstream pop culture that everyone knows about.

But, one of the biggest differences between the movies and the books is that the movies don't spend hours telling you about the world the characters are interacting in.

The question is, are the settings really all that different? Is there more drama and action and story in the movies? Possibly. But, the climaxes were the same. Each just had a different way of setting that climax up. And, let's be very clear about this: Lord of the Rings needed to have that climax set up for it.

Imagine for just a moment that you heard a story about a midget who climbed up a volcano to throw away a ring, and then decided against it. In a big surprise, a sneaky little anorexic midget jumps on him and bites off his finger, plunging himself and the ring into the lava below.

Is that an epic story? Not really. It's kind of weird. It leaves you with all kinds of questions. Why did he want to get rid of the ring? Why did he have to throw it into a volcano to get rid of it? Why was he a midget? Why was the other midget anorexic? The list goes on.

There is nothing epic about that story. There is no struggle for the future of the world. There is no clash between good and evil. We don't even care about who the characters are.

But, by reading the book or watching the movie, you learn the answers to those questions. You learn what a "Hobbit" is, and just how evil the One Ring actually was. As you write, think about the questions that people might have about your story. What details do you need to set up so that the ending makes sense?

The climax is a powerful moment, but a good setting is the reason *why* it is powerful. Take the time to make sure your reader understands enough to make the climax that moment you want it to be.

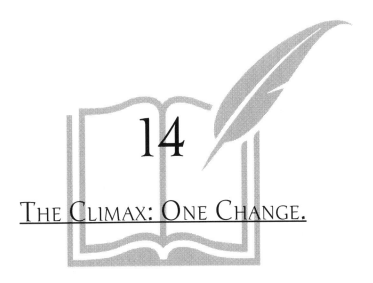

14

THE CLIMAX: ONE CHANGE.

Climaxes are in essence, the punchlines of the drama genre. And a good climax needs exactly one thing: A Change.

A climax is the moment when something *happens*. It is that moment when your best friend actually moves away. It's the moment when you take a stand. It's the moment when you learn a lesson. You might think that an action movie is all climax, but it's not. It sets up the status quo, and why all of the action needs to happen. Then, the characters all work hard to make that big change, whether it be stopping the bad guy's evil satellite, or finally stopping his reign of terror. None of it *matters* without the climax.

Now, we need to clarify something. Remember earlier when I said that most people don't live in a typical story plot? We each have cycles of ups and down, and our lives don't resemble that nice little mountain diagram. However, this doesn't mean that there are no climaxes. In fact, I'll bet you can think of a few of those pivotal moments in your life right now. Remember your Turning Points exercise? Those are climaxes.

Now look at the other stories you've chosen. None of them are about a day that you just woke up and then went to sleep at the end of it with nothing eventful happening in between. What happened that made that time special? When you look at the story, what is the "punchline?" What is the moment you are trying to get to? Why do you want to tell that story?

Look at the key moment of each of those memories that you wrote down. Can you see what changed? If you're still having trouble, don't worry. It's there. If there weren't a change, you wouldn't care about telling it. In fact, chances are that it falls into one of the following categories:

You Changed

Because of an experience, you changed the way that you thought about things, or changed the way you live your life. These climaxes are usually the result of a journey of some sort or another. The climax comes when you achieve something, or when something forced you to be different.

This might look like long years of training to become the best Thai Kickboxer in the world, or when you finally quit your job and started your own business. It might be when you got into that car accident that left you paralyzed, or when your wife was diagnosed with cancer (big changes in our loved ones often reflect in ourselves as well). These climaxes mark transitions between phases in your life. Sometimes, the story simply marks the experiences that lead to the *decision* to change.

The World Changed

Some events are really life changing. This is not because you saw something differently or learned a lesson (although those might happen as well). The climax happens because there was some fundamental shift in the world.

Examples of this include events like Pearl Harbor or 9/11. If you go further back, it could be as simple as the one to immigrate from their home to a whole new world somewhere else. These are events that show who you are because of what you lived through. When writing a history, painting yourself into one of these moments creates a powerful sense of connection for the reader. You are no longer just a name in a list of ancestors. You were the one who lived through a specific event, and were influenced by it.

Note that it could also include lesser known events that changed the world. The death of a parent or losing a job can be just as impacting on a personal scale as the Great Recession was to the world economy.

You Noticed a Change

Sometimes, a climax comes because you finally *noticed* a change, and that changed you. Something unexpected shifted the way that you saw things. In these climaxes nothing in the world actually changed, but you are changed because you can now see it clearer, or differently.

My story about my best friend was one of these climaxes. Note that in that example, I didn't instantly change myself. When my friend moved, it didn't turn me into a hero. Rather, thinking about his absence revealed to me the characteristic that I had been building the whole time. Then, once I noticed it, I was able to confidently step into a new role. The change had been slow, but the climax was when I *saw* it.

Before we move on, there is one point that needs to be addressed: Not all climaxes are good. Some stories don't have a happy ending. Sometimes, we learn the wrong lesson. Before you throw these stories out, consider this: the terrible punchlines that life throws at us, serve to emphasize your humanity, and can be a lesson to those who follow.

If you want, you can certainly paint a picture of yourself or your ancestor as a gallant, epic figure riding into the sunset. Your history is what you want it to be. But, before you go saddling up, I would recommend taking a look at those dark moments in your life. While it is tempting to glaze over your mistakes and emphasize your glory days, it also estranges you from your reader.

Every single person to read your book will have made errors in their own life. They will have make mistakes and stumbled. By showing your own, you will give your reader something to relate to. You become human. When your shining moments are the only thing that show up, people mistakenly assume that your character prevented you from making them; you never messed up because it just wasn't in you.

When you show your dark moments as well as the shining ones, you succeed in spite of your faults. You teach the consequences of bad decisions in a way that is real, and even painful. But, it also gives hope and shows your ability to be better than your worst moments. Please be willing to tell the *whole* story.

15

THE MORAL: WHY IT MATTERS

You might have noticed that this particular part of the story isn't mentioned in the map of how a story is supposed to play out. There's no particular place that you're supposed to put it. It seems obvious that the moral would go into the tail end of one of Aesop's Fables, but it's not so obvious where it should go in the regular stories you tell grandkids about, "When I was your age…"

So why include a moral?

In writing a memoir, you have the chance to do more than just chronicle your life. Like I've said before, it is not a biography. We're frankly not interested in all of the in's and out's of your dating life as a teenager, or the particular struggles of your wife's third pregnancy. It's not that those things weren't dramatic or painful at the time. It's that in the long run, we need to answer one question with each of the stories you choose to include:

So what?

Please don't take this to be impertinent or disrespectful. It's not. One of the best pieces of advice I've ever read about writing said that the reader does not turn the page so they can applaud at the end. The meaning behind this is both more simple and more complex than you might realize.

First off, it means that your book, your memoirs, are not a performance. You don't have a guaranteed captive audience. You have single readers. Each person will read your book and experience it individually. There will be no laugh track in the background to cue them to what is funny, and no dramatic soundtrack to tell them when things are getting serious. You must tell them what is important.

Second, you must realize that your reader will continue

to read your book, not because they want to tell you how good it is, but because they are getting something out of it. It might be a few nuggets of wisdom, or just a great story. Maybe they really want to connect with an ancestor and hear about their life. Regardless, your reader will turn the page because they are getting something.

So, when I say moral, I don't mean that you must always include a mushy life lesson that shows how your life was just full of clichés. The moral is just the part where you make the story applicable to the reader. It's the part where you relate your story, and actually create the connection.

So now the real question. How do you do that? Well, there are a few ways:

The Life Lesson

Just because it doesn't have to be a big life lesson doesn't mean that it can't be one either. Feel free to be corny and say what you learned from the story. If you learned that you can't trust everyone you meet on the street, say it. If you've been choosing the right stories, then your moral should be something that you lived the rest of your life by, or that significantly impacted the way that you think. It stuck out in your mind for a reason. Now you just have to write it down.

Explaining a life lesson doesn't need to be heavy and absolute, either. It could be as simple as stating that you've found that life simply works a particular way, or that a particular rule has served you well.

Work on relating this lesson back to the story using emotional connections to avoid coming across as preaching. You could try something like:

> *Making that decision was hard, and life wasn't very easy for a few weeks afterwards, but my integrity was worth it. I am better because of it.*

Tongue-in-Cheek morals

To speak tongue-in-cheek means to speak in a way that is characterized by insecurity, irony, or whimsical exaggeration. If you don't feel like getting too heavy handed with your advice, try a more jovial tone. For many people, it is a lot easier to teach this way because they it doesn't sound like they are condemning those who don't agree with them.

This can be done by understating the moral:

Remembering the 12 car pile up that I caused gave me a slight pause the next time I thought about texting and driving.

It can also be done following humorous stories to emphasize just why they were so funny:

It just goes to show, you actually can teach an old dog new tricks, as long as you don't mind the dog using his walker to do them.

Regardless of how you write up your morals, what they tell your reader is something very important: I grew up.

Your morals explain that you actually gained experience from your experiences. They weren't just things that happened to you. They meant something, and you were better because of them.

This is the part where you sit down and actually finish writing your B.U.D. I know it's a challenge, but it's time to do it. You've gotten some counsel on how to improve your writing, but before you get to worried about following all of it, just write it all down.

In fact, I forbid you to read any further until you have at least written your B.U.D. (that is, as much as any author can forbid his reader from continuing). Just like before, I promise that I'll still be here when you get done. But, if you don't write it down now, when will you? So fold down the page and I'll talk to you when you're done.

PART 4

BRINGING OUT THE BEST

16

EDITING

So you've finished your B.U.D. The Big Ugly Draft is done. If you're like some writers I have met, then you might be tempted to think that you're there. Just a few minor tweaks and copies of your book will magically appear on your bookshelf.

Nope.

Sorry to burst your bubble, but there's much, much more. The truth is that you might be halfway done... Maybe.

The whole reason why the BUD exists in the first place is to get you writing so that you have something to edit.

Because editing is where the *real* magic happens.

But wait. Why did I have you write out all of that before? Why did I teach you all of that stuff about showing and not telling ahead of time if you're just going to chop it up and ruin your beautiful experience?

Because I have a secret to tell you: Editing is much more magical (and fun) than anyone ever told you.

When I was in middle school, and my dad was editing my papers, I had a very clear picture in my mind of what I thought editing meant. I saw myself print out a masterpiece that I sweated and labored over (for a whole hour) just to have him rip it to shreds. When he was done marking it with red ink, I would take the poor, bleeding paper back downstairs and try again.

At the time, it felt like each strike with the pen was another barrier placed in front of me, separating me from the moment when I would be able to collapse into the comforting embrace of my bed. I *knew* that editing pens were red to simulate my blood that the editor wished he could actually spill.

The truth was that I had procrastinated. I thought that you just wrote a paper and turned it in. I thought that my first drafts were so amazing that they didn't need anything else. My B.U.D. was, in my mind, a perfect representation of my soul. So when anything criticized my paper, I took it personally.

But, as I wrote more, there was something about editing that began to grow on me. And because of that, I want you to have a different view of the editing process. We're going to call it something different altogether. We're going to call it:

Iteration

Iteration is a mathematical term that is used to describe a process used to get closer and closer to a final solution. Each time the process is repeated, the outcome is closer to what you actually want or need. What that means for us is that your B.U.D. is an approximation. The first approximation, technically. It's not quite what you want your book to be. And, each round of editing is going to take it one step closer to what you actually want to send out there.

But, how does iteration work?

Well, like I mentioned, you start off with a basic idea. Then, you give it to someone else and get their take on it. You used their ideas to improve on it, creating a new, better idea. In our case, we are going to be using iteration to work on a book, but it has been used for everything from computer code to music.

For example:

Have you ever heard the song Hallelujah? Chances are you've heard the hit version by Jeff Buckley in 1994. But, it's a cover! It was an iteration of something that was already out there. The version he heard and copied was performed by John Cale. Jeff heard the song because he happened to be house-sitting at a house that had a copy of the Cale album with the song. But, the version he copied wasn't even the original.

The original was written by Leonard Cohen way back in 1983. He had over 80 verses written down to the song, and the version he played on tour depended on what he felt like singing. John Cale happened to hear a version of it one night in a club and asked if he could cover it. Cale's cover version got recorded, and that recording was the one in the house where Jeff Buckley was staying.

Leonard had hundreds of iterations of the song. John Cale brought a new iteration of the song and then Jeff Buckley another. And, since then, hundreds of artists have covered it, each adding their own little bit of style.

Today, we acknowledge the song as a masterpiece, but it was not received as such. Cohen's version was not particularly inspiring, and Cale's version was meant as a tribute to Cohen. Buckley's version might never have been made famous were it not for his untimely death. But, now, because of all of the covers, all of the iterations, it is a magnificent song.

This doesn't mean that your book is going to be rewritten hundreds of times by different authors. It does mean that your book will benefit significantly from rewriting it, and showing it to others.

By the time you get to your final draft, the one you want to send off to be published, you will have something you can be proud of. So let's get on to the good stuff, shall we?

17

TAKE A STEP BACK

When you've finished your B.U.D., you could have the same tendency that many authors have to think you have just hand crafted the most beautiful thing ever. You might not even see what needs to be corrected. I could tell you to not believe it, but in my experience, there's only one thing that will accent the Big and Ugly parts of your draft.

You need to take a break.

When you've finished your Big Ugly Draft, set aside a week or so to leave it alone. Don't touch it. You'll want to go back and read it or tell others you're finally "done" with your book, but I'm begging you: don't.

First, like I've already said, you're not "done" with your book. Not even close. And second, when you get done with that week or so that you've taken off, you're going to see your writing in a whole new light. In the meantime, it's ok to take some time and celebrate. Getting that B.U.D. done is a lot of hard work and you deserve a good old pat on the back or whatever reward you might like.

When you've taken some time off, return to your book, but this time, you're going to shift the way you look at it. To write the B.U.D., you needed a "just get through it" mentality. Now it's time to start thinking with an "iteration" mentality like we talked about earlier. Now, as you look at your book, it's time to get really excited.

Writing the B.U.D. was like getting a set of legos and building that first model. It looks really cool, but the real fun is just beginning. Iterating your book is going to be the part where you take it apart and make it even better.

Just remember that as you edit, you might have the tendency to slip back in close to the B.U.D., and getting attached to it again. If you find yourself feeling defensive about it, or unable to find anything to correct, take another day off. It is crucial that you take as much of an objective view of the iteration process as you can.

This doesn't mean that you shouldn't care about your book anymore. Don't you dare go thinking that you can just "not care" about it. You need to care. The difference is that before, your priority was to recreate your experience for your reader. Now, your goal has shifted. Your goal now is to optimize that story. It is to make the experience as powerful as possible for your reader.

In her book "Everybody Writes," author Ann Handley calls this process being "pathologically empathic" with your reader. I love the idea of working "pathologically" hard to get into your readers head.

But, before you can do that, you must take a step back and first get out of your *own* head so that you can do what is necessary. Be willing to let your stories grow into the book your reader needs.

Your Reader's Group

The last thing you should do is get together a group of people to read your book. Note that I do not mean get around a campfire and read the final copy. A readers group is a group of people you will give manuscripts to so they can read it and tell you what they think. Find some people who will be willing to give your stories a couple of reads, because you will be going back to them.

18

GET A TEAM

When you are editing, please don't try to do it alone. There are things you will miss, and mistakes you won't catch.

Instead, start now to build an editing team. The old saying goes that two heads are better than one. When it comes to writing and especially editing a book, this goes double. One of the greatest challenges to writing your own book is that you are too close to the stories in it. You lived them. You *know* what they mean. But that doesn't mean your reader does.

One of the biggest lessons I have learned while ghost

writing for others is that there are coincidences they didn't even notice, and questions they didn't think to even ask. It's not because the authors were faulty as writers or as storytellers. It didn't mean that their memories were lacking. There were just details that they left out because they were so familiar with them.

Imagine, for example, what the story of Rosa Parks would have meant if she had neglected to mention that she was black. She knew she was black. It was something that she lived with every day, but if you were to try and write her story and leave out that fact, it would come across as strange. Some people could make the connection, but the few that couldn't would fail to see a moment that catalyzed a movement. Or, imagine for a moment trying to understand the story without the knowledge of Jim Crow laws dictating where people could sit on the bus. Little details can make a big difference.

For this reason, it is important to get a team together that can help you see these gaps and get them into your story.

On the other side, there might be details that you consider to be essential that really add almost nothing to the overall story or even confuse things. Your team can help you spot those bits and make sure they get cut.

So who should be on your team?

If you can afford to get a professional editor or two, do it. The professional editors know what their job is, and they will tell you in no uncertain terms what needs to change. Their rates vary, but you can find a decent one on websites like Fiver.com or elance.com. Simply go to the site and type in book editor.

If you'd rather not go that route, at least find someone with some experience working in writing or editing. It can be a friend or family member, but make sure they know what they are doing with the language.

Copy editor

The most basic editor you will need is a copy editor. This just means someone who will look through your book to check for your grammar, punctuation, and word usage. Their job is to make sure that you used the right form of there, their, or they're, and that you didn't say "could of" instead of "could have."

When looking for a copy editor, you probably don't need to look any further than the person at your Thanksgiving table who last turned to their child to tell them, "Superman does good, dear. You are doing well." Find a person who has opinion about the Oxford comma and cringes a little when they hear a made up word for the first time. If those don't mean anything to you, trust me, it will to them.

Content Editor

You'll also need a content editor. In this person, the most important thing you can find is honesty and clarity. Your content editor will look at your book and help you make it better from a "story" point of view. He or she should be asking questions like:

- This is awkward. What might be a better way to say this?

- Have you thought about changing this to…?

- What are you trying to say here?

- Could we try doing…?

The reason honesty is so important here is that they need to be able to talk to you without hurting your feelings. They can't be afraid of how you might react when they suggest an edit. Their goal is to play with the book until it's better, teasing out the real meaning of your stories.

If they're going to be honest, though, then you are going to need to learn a new skill as well: Patience.

Like we've already talked about, you need to take a big step back when handling your book. Understand that your team is there to make things better, not worse. They are not attacking you personally by suggesting changes. They are looking out for you.

Lastly, as helpful as all of the different types of editors are, the best thing you can do is to give copies of your book to the type of people you want to read it. If that includes family, get them together to read it!

Don't worry about surprising everyone with your book as a Christmas present. It will mean a lot more to them if they get to be part of the process than if you were to just give them a mediocre book.

You'll also find that by including these people in your editing process, you'll run into details that you might have forgotten or never known about. Those details will help to fill out the book and make it complete in the eyes of all the people reading it.

Perhaps the biggest reason why you should get a readers group is to make sure that your book is doing all that you want it to do.

Is your book supposed to be funny? Your readers will either laugh or they won't. Is it supposed to be inspiring? Your readers will let you know. Is your book supposed to make sense? Watch out for that confused look on their faces.

In the end, your book is not about you. It is about them. I've said it before, but it deserves to be repeated: your book is for your reader. Having a team gives you a small scale example of whether or not you are reaching the people you want to talk to. They remove the doubt that you might have had and can tell you if your book is interesting or not.

As a last note, you will probably get suggestions from your readers. They might have things they want to change or bits they wish were in there. They might want you to leave out some pieces. This input in very valuable.

Listen to what your readers say, but don't be ruled by it. The choice is yours what to include. In the end, your goal should not be to please everybody. It should be to communicate with them. You can make concessions here and there if they don't change the story, or to make things clearer. But don't shy away from telling a story or part of one because it doesn't paint everything as perfect. Your book is there to tell them who you are and what you do. Don't change that just because someone doesn't like it.

CONNECT WITH YOUR READER.

It can be tempting to write a big long book that describes in detail every aspect of your life. You might be tempted to write poetry or make your writing super flowery to try and make it stand out. Before you do, there is one thing you should remember:

"The reader doesn't turn the page because of a hunger to applaud." - Don Murray

In other words, stop trying to impress everyone. When I started writing, I thought I needed to use big words and convoluted sentences to get my point across. Now I know that connecting with the reader is more important than their opinion of my intelligence.

You won't be reading your book in front of an audience. Even if you do, that experience will be the exception, and not the rule. Don't try to impress them. Try to connect.

What's the difference?

When you try to impress someone, you make a fatal mistake. You express one thing: this is about me. To be fair, you may very well be a very impressive person. In my experience, just about everyone has a story that would make your jaw drop if you knew it. But, that doesn't mean that we're all going to clap for you and pay to go to a concert where you tell it.

On the other hand, connection is all about *him* or *her*. Note that I could have said them, but didn't. This is because people will be reading your book one at a time. It is an individual experience that they will each have as the words you wrote go into their brains. Don't make this about you. When they read your book, let him or her get something out of it, and remove as many barriers as you can between yourself and your reader.

Want to hear an interesting example of this principle? It's about a guy name Paul.

Paul was a pretty smart guy, and wrote some of the most influential letters that the world has ever seen. He traveled the world teaching people about his experiences. But, one story of his always struck me as a little strange.

It's about circumcision.

It's not super popular to talk about today, but circumcision was a big deal during Paul's time. It was a major part of what it meant to be a Jew, and so when Paul and the other Christians started teaching, they ran into some interesting questions regarding the whole order of events around circumcision.

After all, the first Christians and Jesus were all Jews before they were Christians. They had already been circumcised. But, now, there were some non-Jews who wanted to be Christians, and nobody knew if they had to be circumcised first or not.

The argument got pretty heated, and reached the top levels of church government, before Paul finally came out with a solid definitive argument against it. He said, No, and it was the final answer.

I'm not going to go into the theology, but Paul's answer was good enough. Circumcision wasn't necessary to be a Christian, or get into heaven.

But, there's a twist in the story. Paul was going to preach to a bunch of Jews and was going to take a Greek friend with him. They were preparing for their trip when Paul turned to him and recommended that he get circumcised.

Wait a sec.

Didn't Paul just say that it wasn't necessary? Why would his friend need it? Today, getting circumcised as a full grown man is not a pleasant process, but it was much worse then. So what was the point?

I can tell you this much, it wasn't to impress the Jews. It wasn't so that the Greek could strut his stuff around and fit in. It was to connect with them. He did this by removing the barriers, and taking away objections.

What does this have to do with your writing? Everything.

If you want to really connect with your readers, it means that you need to remove all of the barriers between you as you can. It means learning to bend over backwards to make yourself accessible, even if you think it's not necessary.

That whole phrase "when in Rome, do as the Romans" was coined by Paul to explain that you don't get any extra brownie points for being hard to understand, or obnoxiously off-putting. The only thing that counts is publishing a book people will actually read.

To be clear, you could very easily write up a book and publish it without caring at all about the people who read it. I've read more than a few books that do just that. They pretend to be informative, but are really just thinly disguised attempts by the author to show off their knowledge. The tomes are barely readable.

And that's not to say that the information is bad. It's just that in today's world, *how you say it* is just as important as *what* you are saying.

In other words, as you edit your book, work hard to keep your reader in mind. You wrote them down without worrying about them, and these are *your* stories, but you are giving them to someone *else*. Use your readers group to as a testing ground. Make this a gift they can read and accept.

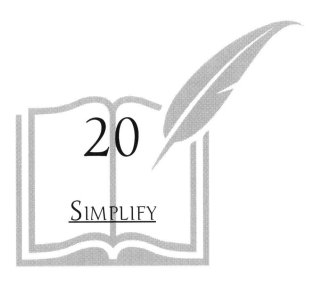

20

<u>SIMPLIFY</u>

Tim Ferriss, an author I very much admire, has a large knife with the word "SIMPLIFY" in all caps underneath it. It serves as a constant reminder to him to work to simplify his writing and his life.

You started out by writing down your stories. I told you all of the methods to make them nice and detailed. I explained to you how to "show" and not "tell". That advice might make this section seem out of place. Stick with me, though, because this is going to make your writing great.

When I say simplify, what I really mean is two specific skills that you should keep in mind as you edit your draft.

As you learn them, plan on running through of your draft two more times, focusing on each one separately. Each will improve drastically the quality of your writing.

Get specific

When you write, try to condense the words you are using. Did you write 'big golden dog that loves to play fetch?' Let's just call him a 'golden retriever' and move on. Showing is much more about being concise than it is about taking up space with description. Only mention fetch when it is actually relevant to the story. Bringing in the little details is important, but be precise with them.

If your first car was a maroon Astrovan (like mine was) that you called the Deathstar (which we did), then put in a quick sentence about it, and then you can all pile into the Deathstar instead of getting into the car. From that point on, the word 'Deathstar' describes your car, and gives it character, all in one little word.

Be specific, but also be careful not to bury your reader in techno-babble. Letting the reader know that it was a maroon astrovan is fun, but they don't need to know that it was a '92 Astrovan, Luxury Touring model. You can say you had a cool 'RAZR' flip phone, but we don't need the serial number, or the specs. Likewise, you can say that when your car broke down, it had transmission problems, without going into details about the abrupt shift from first to second gear that tends to manifest at around 48,000 miles in Astrovans.

Use specifics to enhance the story and give it character, but avoid bogging things down with needless description. As you go through your B.U.D., look for descriptions you could condense and places where one word would work better than many. Consciously work to decide which details are there, and what they add to the story.

Start cutting

I've noticed a funny trend in the movie industry. Directors make the theatrical cut of their film, designed to be shown in theaters. Then, when they come out with the movie to buy on BluRay or DVD, you can pay a little extra for the "director's cut." Yet, in my experience, what that term, "director's cut" really means is: We stuck a few extra minutes of film into the movie that were so essential, that they got rid of it the first time around. Seems kind of strange, right?

If those moments really were so good that the director wanted them included in his "cut" of the movie, why weren't they shown in theaters? Don't follow that trend.

Don't plan on making a "director's cut" of your book. It won't make it to BluRay, and trust me when I say that bloopers in a book are much less entertaining than the ones in a movie. Make one version of your book, and cut out the extra. Don't be afraid of getting rid of the junk.

I know of a writer who regularly had the first two paragraphs of each paper chopped off by her editor. He would just go in and delete them. After a while, she learned to just get to the story and not take her time weaving around to it.

The point of cutting is to get rid of the stuff that doesn't add to the story. When you are editing your story to cut out the extra, there is one question that you should be asking constantly:

What would the story be like without this?

If you were to cut the paragraph you just read, could it survive? What would it be like? Rather than asking if it adds, try actually subtracting and seeing if the story feels any different. Sometimes, you'll have a huge hole in the story. Sometimes, it'll just be a small one. And, sometimes, you won't even notice. If your story feels the same without it, maybe you don't need it.

And, the parts that ended up on the "cutting room floor?" Leave them there. Your book will be better without them.

Don't be afraid to be merciless. Throughout the editing process, you'll end up adding more in anyway. We want your book to be as good as possible, and not just fill the pages.

PART 5

MAKING IT REAL

21

LAYOUT AND FORMATTING

Now we get into the more boring bits and pieces of the whole process. I say boring because this is likely where you will start to tire with writing your book. You've written a draft. You've iterated it time and time again until you feel like you've got it right, or at least as close as it's going to get. So what's next? Getting your book ready for print.

The truth is that you probably will need someone to help you with the next bit: Layout and formatting.

Layout and formatting are what take your words and make them look like a book. Right now, you have a manuscript (that's what a book is called before it gets formatted). You might think it could probably just get shoved into a program and it all pops out as an ebook or in printing format, but unfortunately, it's a little more complicated than that.

While I could go into a conversation about formatting tips and fonts, spacing, book sizes and all of that, I won't. Your formatter should help you with that. Yes, I am *highly* recommending finding someone like me for this part.

You see, formatting and layout are both learned skills, and are usually done inside of a nice piece of software specifically designed for it. When I tried to layout my first book using Microsoft Word, it was way more hassle than it was worth. And, even when I did get it all said and done, it still didn't look very professional. In fact, it mostly just looked like someone had printed out a Word document and pasted a cover onto it.

The second time I published a book, I still felt like doing it myself. So I spent countless hours learning how to use Adobe's premier software, InDesign. The software required a good computer, and a subscription to use it. Then, after I learned how to use the software, I needed to spend *more* hours learning what actually looks good and how to implement it. I took classes on fonts, character types, spacing, tracking, letting and a whole bunch of other terms that publishers throw around like it's no big deal.

In the end, the book looked great, but it was exhausting to get it there. The time I spent working on it could have been cut way down if I had just found a good typesetter to do it for me. I don't regret the time spent learning how to do it all, but then, I'm also in the business of helping people publish books. The long courses aren't for everyone, and typesetters are not that expensive.

At this point, even knowing what I know, I'll do both. Sometimes, I'll go in and layout the book myself, opting for the flexibility and specificity that comes with designing my own book. In general, though, it's easier to find someone to do it for me. Costs are generally a few dollars a page, and their work will take *significantly* less time than yours, and look better.

Now, it may be that you have always secretly wondered exactly how print publishers layout their books and posters and other materials so that they look so good. If that's the case, feel free to take some classes. There are a lot of sites online that could help you with the learning part of it, and it can be fun if you like that sort of thing.

But, for the average person whose goal is to publish a book, and not to spend weeks learning a new skill, I'd recommend finding someone to do it for you. And, this might be a moot point if you choose a publisher that includes layout in the deal. For simple layout, I'd recommend using a site like upwork.com or fiverr.com to find a relatively cheap typesetter.

If you want to make things really easy, I've put together a package to get your book laid out and formatted without you needing to do much at all. You'll send me your manuscript and I'll do a basic formatting and layout and get it published on Amazon.com. You can check out that option on my website: www.EstoriaPress.com.

The Finicky Bits

Something you should know before you start looking at layout and formatting, let alone publishing, is that different publishers have different capabilities.

You might want your book to be a little pocket book that you can hand out to people. If that's the case, you'll need to look into publishers to make sure that the one you want to use has the size that you want. You'll want to check into paper quality, whether or not you are going to use color, and whether your book will be hardbound or soft bound. You'll want to consider how many copies of your book you will be printing, and whether you want to print them and sell them yourself or work through someone else. Different publishers offer different things, and you at least have a rough idea of what you are looking for before your layout person starts their work.

Making sure that your layout person knows what you are shooting for is essential to getting what you want out of your book. Otherwise, you could end up with a format that is half an inch too short for the book, causing a stretch in the final printing, or a font that is microscopic and requires a magnifying glass. Be specific with what you want from your book.

The best way to go about this is to take a moment before you start formatting but after your manuscript is done. Ask yourself, what do I imagine the final project will look like? Then write that down. Try sketching out what you think the book will look like. Imagine holding it in your hands.

Try to answer the following questions:

- How big will it be? What dimensions? Check against standard book sizes.

- What will it look like to flip through the book? Will there be color?

- Will there be pictures? If so, where?

- What will it look like on the back? Pictures? Testimonials? A summary?

- What will the cover look like? A single picture? A specific design?

- What quality will the book be? Thin, light and cheap to print? Sturdy and meant to last?

- Will the book be hardcover or softcover?

Once you have the answer to these questions, check the publishing site you plan on using to make sure they can do what you are asking of them. Can they make a hardbound book in your size? In color? Check first to make sure your publisher can make the book you envision. If not, consider shifting publishers. I have shifted publishers for things as simple as the timeframe I could expect the book in.

Then, once you have a publisher that can print what you want, make sure you send all of your specifications (yours and the publisher's) to your layout person. I cannot stress enough that you work on getting the specifications nailed down first. This will prevent a lot of extra work on the formatter's part, and a lot of grief later on.

22

Designing a Book Cover

Once you have your book laid out and formatted, there's just one thing left to make it a book: the cover. The process of designing a book cover will be exactly as difficult as you decide it needs to be. It can be a time-consuming process that takes a lot of hard work and deep thought, or as simple as thinking up a generic title so you can get it out there. Let's look at the different things you can do and the steps each one can take.

Title

You might find it suspicious that I haven't had a section on naming your book yet. You've probably already found a title that you like and are running with it. I'm not going to dissuade you from it. Your title is whatever you want it to be.

If you want to sell your book to more people, you can do what a lot of different amateur authors do: Go to Amazon.com and find some examples of the best-selling books in your category (in this case, look for memoirs or biographies) and look at the titles. Then, make a title that sounds like theirs. As of this writing, the top five most popular memoirs are:

- Born a Crime, Stories from a South African Childhood (by Trevor Noah)

- Hillbilly Elegy: A Memoir of a Family and Culture in Crisis (by J. D. Vance)

- The Magnolia Story (by Chip and Joanna Gaines with Mark Dagostino, who was likely their ghostwriter)

- Settle for More (by Megyn Kelly)

- Scrappy Little Nobody (by Anna Kendrick)

As a side note, two of them are audiobooks, three are hardcover books, and the sixth place entry is the ebook version of one of the first five. That will mean more to you in the next chapter, but keep it in mind for when we get there.

So what do those titles have in common? Each one is designed to be poignant and specific to the person it's about.

If you're not super concerned about the title, you can do what a lot of people do, and just use their own name as the title of their book. Throw on a subtitle that gives them a taste of your stories. In fact you could just use the following template:

First and Last Name

A story of _____, _____, and _____.

Simple, right? You'd be surprised at just how many people use this format. It works.

Cover

Next, there's your cover. Designing it is exactly as complicated as you want it to be. If you want to take an easier route, put a picture of your face on it, and your title underneath it. It doesn't need to be more.

If you do want more, you can either find a designer to work on one for you, or use a site like 99designs.com to get a bunch of different ideas. Either way, plan on spending a few hundred dollars to pay your designer. When working with them, make sure you are very specific about what you are looking for. The changes are rarely as big as you think they are, and it is much better to have a design you like, and take some time with it, than to rush it and want the tweaks after it is too late.

The Amazon.com trick works well, again, if you are looking for a way to imitate best-selling trends. One thing to remember when designing your cover is that old cliche, don't judge a book by its cover, is wrong. People will judge your book by the way it looks before they ever read it. Putting in a little bit of effort and getting some feedback could go a long way.

23

Publishing Mediums

Let's talk about the final step to take your book from a bunch of digital ones and zeroes, and turning them into a physical book that you can give away, or that others can buy. That means publishing.

To really talk about publishing, though, we have to look at the two major decisions that you have to make. The first is regarding medium, which is just a fancy way of saying how you want people to use your book. The second is publishing options, which we'll talk about in the next chapter.

Electronic

Ebooks are quickly becoming a very popular way to consume literature. To put it simply, an ebook is available for people to read in digital format using an ebook reader, like Kindle or Apple Books. These programs allow for people to carry your book with them anywhere they have an internet capable device. While some complain about the lack of a physical item to hold in their hands, there is an undeniable convenience to being able to carry it with you anywhere without the extra weight.

Audiobook

Another way that books are being transmitted these days is in the audiobook format. These books are basically just a recording of someone reading your book out loud. This format is preferred by some people because it allows them to be doing other things while they get the information. Some listen to podcasts (like radio shows, but downloaded episode by episode) and audiobooks during their morning and evening commute to and from work. Others listen while they workout, or do household chores. If you would like to make your book available as an audiobook, look into publishers like audible.com to help you with the process.

Print

Print books have been around for much much longer than even the printing press. In ancient Egypt, priests wrote on scrolls made of papyrus, and the ancient Chinese created what we know today as paper. Today, bibliophiles will tell you that there will always be something about holding a physical book in your hand.

The advantage to having an actual print book is that it is something physical. You don't have to worry about your readers accessing their account to get it. And if the internet were to ever go out, your book would still be around. On a more practical note, a book on a bookshelf gathers more attention than a digital one does, and a physical gift of a book means more to most than access to a digital copy of something. It's much more exciting to unwrap a book than it is to get an email notification.

So what would I recommend? Probably a bit of both.

If you can manage it, put in the extra work to make sure your book is available no matter how pour readers want to get to it. If you've got a good reading voice, you might consider doing the audiobook yourself as a way to give a personal touch to those who want to listen to it.

24

CHOOSING A PUBLISHER

Your publisher is the person who is going to print and distribute your book. They are the ones in charge of getting your book out there, and selling it.

Like I said at the beginning, my goal is not to teach you how to make a truckload of money by writing, so I'm not going to go into that side of it. However, the publisher you choose will determine how you make money from your book. Different publishers offer different streams of income, from a direct payment or advance to a royalty on the books themselves. You'll need to look into how your publisher structures payment (or work it out yourself).

But, before you start to worry about getting paid, let's get your book printed. Here, there are really only two avenues for you to go with, but each one has a lot of different options associated with it. In a nutshell, you can go with a big publishing house, or self publishing.

The Big Publishing House

This is the route you go if you want to be on bookshelves across the country. The big publishing houses have connections all over the world and know where and how to sell your book. Subsequently, this is exactly what they will try to do.

These big publishing companies will usually have you go through a whole new round of edits with their own editors and help you layout and design your book. In the end, you'll end up with a compromise that lies somewhere between exactly what you want and what they think will sell. The nice news is that your publisher will probably foot the bill for printing and distributing your book. They'll also take some of the profit, but then, that's what they are in the game for.

But, all of this is making one really big assumption: It assumes you actually get accepted for publication. Getting accepted for publication is tough, and many writers spend years trying to get there.

When it comes to getting published by a big company, the best way to go about it is to get a writing agent who will work with the publishing companies to get your book published. Unfortunately, unless you have already published something, you probably don't have an agent. This means that getting published means submitting your manuscript to as many publishing companies as you can, with a cover letter, hoping that one of them sees enough promise in your premise (because they won't be reading the whole manuscript) to warrant an actual read through.

If you do decide to go the route of the big publishing company, be prepared for a lot of rejection. I don't say this to be harsh, or mean. Realistically, your book will be rejected many times before (and if) you are accepted and published. One of my writing heroes, Tim Ferriss, wrote a New York Times Bestseller that was rejected by 14 different publishers before it got printed.

This might sound discouraging, and it would be if it were the only option. Once upon a time, your choices were to get a big house to publish a book for you, or pay for a huge order out of pocket. Luckily for you (and me) there is another option out there that has sprung up in the last decade that allows for anyone to publish on any scale:

Self Publishing

Self publishing is not nearly as difficult as it might seem. If you've already gone through the rest of the steps in this book, then your book is nearly ready to take to a self publisher right now. Most self publishers don't require much more than a credit card number and a pdf of your book.

Of course, this doesn't make it all rosy either. Self publishing will require you to make more decisions about how you want to publish, and the right publisher who can print a book at the right size and specifications for what you want. Most self publishing companies offer a set of standard sizes and formats that you can publish your book in.

Each company also will have certain requirements as to how they want your final product. Many will accept just a .pdf file, but you still need to figure out how they want your cover (usually a separate file) and some other options like where you will distribute and register your book (ISBN number).

Once you have found someone to actually print the books, you'll want to order a few copies to make sure that they actually print right. Make sure you order test copies before you set them out for sale, or start giving them away.

Reread your test copy, making a last check for typos and problem spots. Does everything look like you thought it would? If not, check with your formatter and fix everything. Sometimes, things simply don't look the same when you physically print them. Remember that the resolution on your computer screen is not necessarily the same as the resolution of your printer. In other words, don't assume that because it looked good when your formatter got done with it, that everything will look perfect on the page.

Continue ordering small numbers of copies until you get ones you are happy with, and then, go big. Put them up on Amazon.com for sale, or print a large batch to sell at your local fair or bookstore. Remember that making a book available is not the same as selling a lot of copies. People have to know about your book before they will buy it.

Keep in mind that in most cases, you will need to pay for the copies that you print. The copies usually cost less as you buy more, but the original costs aren't too high to begin with (under $5 for a 200 page book). They will ship directly to you and you will then be in charge of distribution of them. Selling them is up to you.

25

Self-Publishing Resources

This chapter is designed to be short, but give you some resources to help you get a physical copy of your book into your hands. Each of the resources that I mention here are ones that I have used personally and can recommend based on my experience. They each have their strengths and weaknesses, that I will discuss. However, I also know that not everyone is (or needs to be) a do-it-yourself sort of person. That's why the first self publishing area here is actually my own website and company.

EstoriaPress.com

I know, I know. It's blatant self marketing, but the fact of the matter is that sometimes, you don't want to have to worry about the nitty gritty of it. And, to be perfectly honest, I've worked hard to make this really easy and affordable for you. The most basic service we offer is called the "Publish Me" package, and it takes a lot of the hassle out of the process. Basically, you send us a text document, and we'll do a basic formatting job with it and make it available for you on Amazon. You won't make money on your book, but if all you want is to get it published and available, this is the way to go. I can guarantee that we do this faster than you will be able to, especially if this is your first book, or you've never tried to self publish before. The whole process takes less than a week.

We also offer other packages that will help you with other aspects of the process, including getting a writing coach, and editing services. And, if you've gotten this far and still haven't done much from the first few chapters, we offer comprehensive ghostwriting services so that you don't even have to write the book yourself. Check out our website at www.EstoriaPress.com to see how we can work to make the publishing process easy on you.

That being said, there are other ways to go about getting published. For those who want to go a more DIY route, read on:

LightningSource.com (Ingram Content Group)

This is by far the world's largest self publisher and with good reason. Their specialty is Print On Demand (POD) services. POD means that you don't have to print all of your books at once, hoping that you can get them sold. Instead, the company puts your book up on a number of websites and then prints and ships them to your readers as they buy them. No boxes of books in your garage, waiting to be sold (or ruined by a mistimed flood).

Being the biggest also means that they can do just about anything you could imagine. Want to distribute your book to bookstores in Cardiff, Wales? They could figure it out for you. Want to make sure that copies of your book are available in local libraries? They've got a whole section on it. Any connection that you could want or imagine is most likely available through Ingram.

The cons are simple. With so much available, it can be easy to get bogged down in it all. It's hard to know exactly what you should be doing, and what won't actually give you any benefit. They will assume from the get go that you are going to be publishing a lot. So when they ask if you want a copy of your book on the library shelf in Norway, just remember: they make money by *selling you services*, and not by selling your book. The more services they sell you, the more money they make. And, while they will make some effort to sell you the right services, there might be a difference between what is right for you and right for them.

Another con is that because they are big, their customer service is a little impersonal. They will take care of you, but it might take some time. You should be especially careful when ordering from them around the holidays, as they get swamped and could rush your order at expense of quality.

Lulu.com

This site is great because it can be really easy to get things done. Compared to the other options, it is actually pretty simple. Getting copies of your book can be as easy as uploading the .pdf file of your book and paying a few bucks. When I'm looking to get a quick concept book done, I'll often use something like this.

Lulu can also do the POD like Ingram. In fact, all three of the options I've got here can. I consider that a must in the self publishing business. Nobody wants boxes of unsold books sitting in their garage.

While Lulu can do a lot, it is also designed to be simple. This means that you don't have as many options as far as what happens with your book. That is not to say that you are totally boxed in, because there are still a fair number of ways to go about printing your book. Just be aware that compared to using one of the other sites, Lulu is both the easiest to use, but also the most basic.

CreateSpace.com (Amazon)

While the other publishers can sell through Amazon and connect with the Kindle store (Amazon's ebook seller), CreateSpace has the easiest time doing it. This is because the company is owned by Amazon itself. Using CreateSpace means that your book is automatically printed and shipped by Amazon's factories, and that integration takes no extra effort. POD is included as just a part of what Amazon does.

Additionally, Amazon is probably the best at walking you through the process. They will tell you what you need, and how to upload it (although not necessarily how to get it). Then, they will take you through the process of making your book into an ebook. Of all the systems I've used, CreateSpace wasn't the simplest, but it was the easiest to follow. They also have a lot of different ways to get your book out there (assuming you want to pay a little more to market it).

On the other hand, CreateSpace makes one interesting assumption. They assume that you really aren't going to be selling your book beyond Amazon and some of the bigger stores that Amazon connects with. You could sell it on your own website just fine, but your Uncle's bookstore in Milwaukee might have an interesting time getting it in stock. In Amazon's defense, they are the world's leading bookseller, so even your Uncle could order them from there. This could also be a plus, though, because they can integrate your bank royalties straight into your website and make it easy to get paid. Like the rest of it, there are pro's and cons.

Choosing a self publishing company takes time and research to figure out which is best for you. There are many more out there than just the three I've listed here, and you might find the perfect fit out there somewhere. The most important thing to know when you are looking for a publisher is what you want your final book to look like.

I remember publishing a big coffee table biography for a Manager at Merrill Lynch. We talked about what he wanted, and came up with a product that he liked. One of the things he was looking for was a nice dust jacket to go on his book. But when I started shopping around for publishers, I found something strange. I found many publishers that would do the dust jacket with the book, but the books would be expensive. It wasn't the jacket that was expensive, it was the publishers. The jacket itself was only adding a few dollars to the price of each book. Then I found another publisher that wouldn't do the dust jacket, but could print the books for half of the cost of the other publishers. I took the options to the author, and he chose to go with the jacketless books.

These kind of compromises are common within the publishing world, and finding the right fit will take time.

Different publishers have different options at different prices, and you might not end up with exactly what you want. Don't let this discourage you, though. Figure out what is important in your book, and then make it happen.

26

ADDITIONAL RESOURCES

I've heard it said that writing a book is a lot like having a baby. It's different for everybody, but will likely include some pain and anguish before you get to a good outcome. Writing your memoirs won't be easy, but it will definitely be worth it in the end. With all that being said, the process doesn't have to be super difficult either. There are lots of ways to make this easier on yourself.

One of the biggest things you can do is to find a community of people with the same goal and work with them. If you can't find a group, create one! You can use this book as a starting piece to get you all going. Work through the different exercises and help each other with editing. Having someone to be accountable to will increase your drive to get your book done. Try using sites like meetup. com or Facebook to manage those groups.

If you need more specific advice and instructions, check out EstoriaPress.com. At Estoria Press I have exactly one purpose behind everything I do: to get your stories out into the world. If you find you have more money than time, I can get you a ghostwriter. If you have more time than money, we have easy-to-follow programs that will help take you all the way from idea to finished product.

For other books on writing, I highly recommend *The Elements of Style*, by E. B. White, and *Everybody Writes*, by Ann Handly.

Getting your book published and to the ones you love is important. Take advantage of the resources available at EstoriaPress.com and leave your legacy.

27

WILL YOU DO IT?

I started learning about the person my father really was when I was nearly 20 years old. Yet as late as that seemed, I now realize that there are many people who never get that opportunity. There are people who I have gotten to know only from the outside in. People who I know only because of the people who knew a side of them.

I can't help but wonder what was missing.

For example, I remember that for the last few years of his life, my grandfather lived with us as he began to develop dementia. I knew him as a kind man who would let me ride on his knee. He taught me how to make sounds like a horse galloping by slapping my hands and thighs. I knew he loved me and liked to have me around. I remember his big blue La-Z-Boy chair that sat in our living room. I remember his big smile and the songs he composed and sang to us. I was ten when he died.

My parents remember a different experience. They remember a man who was constantly critical of my own dad. They remember his quirks and general dislike of some of the measures they took to maintain his health. My mom in particular can remember a pretty severe time having to defend my dad from grandpa when he disapproved of something.

Maybe it was because I was young, but it was a side of my grandpa I never heard about until I talked to my parents years later. Maybe they just kept the fighting subdued when I was around. Either way, I am left with a split memory of my grandpa. Half of me sees him as a kind old man who liked to play with his grandkids. The other half sees a critical, bitter old man who berated his son.

But, in spite of all of these memories, I find myself wondering, who would *he* say he was? If he were describing why did what he did with his life, what stories would *he* tell? What kind of person would I discover? What part of him is in me?

I can talk to a lot of people who knew him. I can talk to most of his children. I can talk to his ex-wife, my grandma. Each one of them has a particular opinion and point of view as to who he was. But, when it comes to how the man saw himself, I don't have a lot to go on.

I've learned that he served in the Korean War, and that he was a prolific inventor and electrician. He loved music, and instilled that love in my dad. But what I find myself missing, are the stories.

Many of them died with him.

I mention this, not to terrify or threaten. I mostly just think of my grandpa and wonder. So, what about you?

What stories will follow you to your grave?

In my experience, the pivotal moments in our lives are not the ones that everyone else things were important. They are the ones that everyone else took for granted. I've written a lot in this book about how to write. But, what I hope you take away is something much simpler than a set of tools to write better.

I hope you take with you a commitment to leave behind your own memories.

Of those who bought this book, most will never finish reading it. While I, as the author, appreciate the support, getting more of your money into my pocket was not my goal in writing this book. My goal was to inspire something more.

I want your story to be told.

If you've gotten this far, I hope you'll take this one step further, and commit to yourself to write your memoir. Set a date on the calendar that you want to finish it by. Give yourself a year or so. Use me and my company if you need to. But *please*, if you get nothing else out of this book, commit to writing your story down. I know that you have...

ONE MORE STORY TO TELL.

About the Author

Jason Lee is a writer and the founder of Estoria Press. He is an expert storyteller and loves to share with anyone who will give him the time of day. He enjoys playing all kinds of board games and learned much of his storytelling from playing Dungeons & Dragons as a teenager. Storytelling and playing games turned to writing after high school when he spent two years in Peru on a evangelical mission and then earned a degree in Linguistics from BYU. He and his wife currently reside in Salt Lake City, UT, with their beloved flandoodle, Tiamat.